PRAYERS
of a
PASTOR

PROSPECTIVE PRESS BOOKS BY DON GORDON

Psalms for Children

PRAYERS *of a* PASTOR

Don Gordon

PROSPECTIVE PRESS
CHRISTIAN PUBLICATIONS
Winston-Salem

PROSPECTIVE PRESS
CHRISTIAN PUBLICATIONS

an imprint of
PROSPECTIVE PRESS
1959 Peace Haven Rd #246, Winston-Salem, NC 27106
www.prospectivepress.com

Published in the United States of America by PROSPECTIVE PRESS LLC

PRAYERS OF A PASTOR
Copyright © Don Y. Gordon, 2016
All rights reserved.
The author's moral rights have been asserted.

Author photo © Emily Elrod, 2015

Cover and interior design by ARTE RAVE

ISBN 978-1-943419-32-6

Printed in the United States of America
First edition
First trade paperback printing, December, 2016

1 3 5 7 9 10 8 6 4 2

The text of this book is typeset in Minion Pro
Accent text is typeset in Felipa

EDITOR'S NOTE:

This is a book of prayers—heartfelt messages to God by the author. In order to preserve the tone and tenor of Dr. Gordon's messages, only minimal changes were made to the format of his prayers. Line breaks, indents, singular possessives, and the use of capital letters are as originally written.

PUBLISHER'S NOTE:

This book is a work of poetic non-fiction. The people, names, locations, activities, events, and wording used or implied by this book are a creative endeavor by the author, are used with permission, or are fair use. Any other resemblance to people, locations, events, or works is strictly coincidental.

Without limiting the rights as reserved in the above copyright, no part of this publication may be reproduced, stored in or introduced into any retrieval system, or transmitted—by any means, in any form, electronic, mechanical, photocopying, recording, or otherwise—without the prior written permission of the publisher. Not only is such reproduction illegal and punishable by law, but it also hurts the author who toiled hard on the creation of this work and the publisher who brought it to the world. In the spirit of fair play, and to honor the labor and creativity of the author, we ask that you purchase only authorized electronic and print editions of this work and refrain from participating in or encouraging piracy or electronic piracy of copyright-protected materials. Please give authors a break and don't steal this or any other work.

Cover contains elements © Costin79/Adobe Stock and © kevron2001/Adobe Stock. Used under license.

To all my congregations

Preface

There are two seminal events that have shaped my praying before a congregation of God's people. The first came in a lecture given by Dr. John Carlton, Professor of Worship and Preaching at Southeastern Baptist Theological Seminary, in the spring semester of 1986. This erudite, white-haired man told his class something to the effect, "When you stand up to pray before your congregation, it is as if you are approaching God's glorious throne of grace on behalf of the people. The people have something they want to say to God, and they have chosen you to be their spokesman. You are praying their prayer. You are standing before the throne of God with the people immediately behind you." I have kept that image in mind throughout my thirty years of ministry. It is the main reason I have toiled over my pastoral prayers like many preachers toil over their sermons. My sermons were spoken to the people. My prayers were spoken to God. As the people's representative, I wanted my prayers (their prayers!) to be just as important as the sermon. When preparing to pray to God as the representative of the people, I wanted to review the week, consider the needs of my people, and offer up theologically appropriate petitions and praises, confessions and consolations, thanksgivings and truth-telling.

The second event happened during my doctoral work at Columbia Theological Seminary in Decatur, Georgia in 1999. I was taking a class on the Old Testament under the venerable Dr. Walter Breuggemann. Each day he began his class with a prayer that coincided with the lecture given. It was one of the most profound spiritual experiences of my life. Each class I felt as if I was being ushered into the Holy of Holies before an awesome God. I was terrified, being exposed before this Holy God. Dr. Breuggemann's prayers were so honest, poetic, and poignant as they captured the reality of my sinful heart. And then, in a transitional moment of utter grace, I was surrounded by the love and comfort of this same Holy God. It's hard to imagine how a prayer can be an exhausting and yet exhilarating experience when it lasts only a moment or two. Yet, that was the impact of Breuggemann's prayers on my day, my listening to the lecture, and my future ministry.

For thirty years, I have been writing down prayers and serving as a representative for God's people as they approached his holy throne of grace. Early in my ministry, I was asked by a member of one of my churches, "Why do you write your prayers down? Why not just speak what the Holy Spirit lays on your heart?" I replied, "If the Holy Spirit can speak to my heart on Sunday morning at 11:30 a.m., why can't this same Spirit speak to me Saturday night? There are many people and issues I want to bring to the Lord's attention in my one pastoral prayer of the week. I take that just as seriously as I do the sermon." He seemed satisfied with my answer and never brought the subject to my attention again.

This book is a compilation of some of the prayers that I have spoken—on behalf of my people—before the throne of grace. Many of them will be accompanied by a date and a note regarding the title, theme, or text of the sermon preached that day. I am indebted to Nancy Wooters, a member of my congregation at Yates Baptist Church, for transcribing many of my early prayers from handwritten notes to typed text. I am also indebted to my current congregation, Ardmore Baptist Church, for granting me the time and encouragement to complete this long-awaited effort. Finally, I'm grateful for the editing done by my talented daughter Sarah Gordon Mears, who is putting her English degree to good use. It is my hope that these prayers can serve as a catalyst for pastors who want to recapture the awesome task of approaching a holy God on behalf of a people yearning to be known, heard, and loved by that God, as revealed perfectly through Jesus Christ.

— Don Gordon

Contents

Pastoral Prayers	1
Advent	38
Holy Week	44
World Communion Day	54
All Saints' Day	58
Baptism	60
Missions	62
Commissioning	68
Parent-Child Covenant	70
Ordination	72
Graduation	74
Ten Commandments	78
Marriage and Sexuality	86
Community Senior Citizens Ministry	92
Mother's Day	94
Independence Day	98
Homecoming	100
Organ Dedication	102
Dedication of Town Library	104
Presidential Inauguration	106
Charleston Massacre	110
Invocations	112

Prayers *of a* Pastor

Pastoral Prayers

Almighty God,
We are an ambitious people.
We want you to do for us whatever we ask.
We want rain and expect you to send it.
We want to be great and want you to guarantee it.
We are ambitious about many things.

And then you step out from the whirlwind of your creativity.
You intervene in our lives with your omnipotence.
You reveal to us the pathway of true greatness,
And it goes against the grain of our instincts.
Your revelation stands on servanthood as opposed to power and influence.
So God, show us how to help somebody in need.
Lead us to encourage the downtrodden.
Equip us to be agents of morality without being moralists.
Help us lead by example rather than decree.
Speak your good news in us and through us to the world.
Drive us to greatness in the model of Jesus,
Not through power and wealth, but through service and sacrifice,
Like Jesus our high priest, our best friend, our loving Lord.

Today we remember our sister Susan Denton, whose mother just died,
and Louel Rose, whose husband just died,
and Janet Kindred and Charlie Hege, recovering from surgery.
We ask that you intervene in families where marriages are in conflict
and relations are strained between parents and teenagers.
Bring peace where there is conflict, and kindness where there is tension.
We pray for our family members overseas in places of danger and violence.
We pray for the common people of nations where war and violence are rampant.

Thank you for hearing and answering our prayers,
In Jesus' name. Amen.

A sermon on ambition ~ July 26, 2015

*H*eavenly Father,
We come today as debtors.
We pray daily that you forgive our debts,
And we qualify our prayer by the condition that we forgive our debtors.
We dare pray for the cancellation of all these debts, our own and others.

We pray for the cancellation of the debt of
> our pride, believing we are better than others because of
> our superior intelligence, or wealth, or even religious commitments;
> our idolatries, putting others and other things before
>> Jesus and the kingdom of God;
> our infidelities, living unfaithfully to our spouses, our children
> our friends, and even to you, God.

And we pray with as much fervency that we might forgive
> our debtors,
> our friends who let us down,
> our spouses who betrayed us,
> our children who failed to acknowledge our investment in their lives,
> our church, which let our pain and suffering go unnoticed.

Father, we pray for the cancellation of debts of those who can't pay,
> the poor who have no money,
> third World nations whose infrastructure can't compete in a global economy,
> the slaves whose bodies are owned by evil people and used by ordinary people every day,
> the imprisoned, who are paying their debts, but will really never finish paying their debts.

Father, we are all debtors, trespassers, sinners,
None of us are righteous, no not one.
So we all come today as debtors,
And we praise you for the unbelievable, unimaginable, unfathomable
cancellation of our debts, our trespasses, our sins,
through the blood of our Lord Jesus Christ,
who taught us to pray, saying....

A sermon from the Lord's Prayer ~ April 15, 2015

𝒜lmighty God,
We acknowledge what you know;
> That kingdoms rage on Earth against one another.
> Refugees from Syria flood into Lebanon seeking safety.
> Christians in Egypt are on edge.
> Children in Ethiopia are numb from hunger.

God, we pray for your kingdom come on Earth as it is in heaven.
> Act, Oh God. Speak assurances. Send food.
> Designate your human agents of relief and comfort and peace.
> Right in the middle of this chaos,
>> Act.
>> Intervene.
>> Overthrow evil with good,
>>> prejudice with compassion,
>>> war with peace,
>>> hunger with nutrition.
>> Raise up leaders who will act as your prophets and your messengers.
>> Speak through your chaplains at Forsyth Hospital.
>> Comfort through Rob Lemons at the Ronald McDonald House.
>> Bring peace to regions in the Middle East.

Father take our conflicted world of love in the midst of war, and teach us how to live;
> bringing aid to the refugee and wedding gifts to the young and married,
> offering food to starving children and playing kickball with our own,
> lifting up the downtrodden and rejoicing with those who rejoice.

Temper our schizophrenia of movement between sorrow and gladness,
So that we avoid insanity and act with divine graciousness, mercy, and wisdom.
In all things, the good and bad, let our voices, thoughts, and deeds
> reveal a glimpse of your kingdom on earth, as it is in heaven.

And so we pray....

A sermon on the phrase "Thy kingdom come, thy will be done on earth as it is in heaven"
March 1, 2015

Heavenly Father,
You are the Father of our Savior Jesus.
You are the one he spoke to, so we speak to you.
You are the one he depended on, so we depend on you.
You are the one who guided his steps, so we ask for guidance.

We are unlike Jesus in many ways,
despite the fact we have the same heavenly Father.
> He was faithful, and we are fickle.
> He cleaved to you always, and we leave you when another
> star attracts our attention.
> He was obedient to the end, and we tire of obedience.

We are like the Prodigal Son, gone astray, bored with a life of obedience on the farm.
Still, you are Father to us both, Jesus and us.

You are the Heavenly Father
> who waits on us while we are away,
> who leaves the door unlocked so we can return home,
> who yearns for us to return,
> who goes out to seek us at all hours of the night,
> who loves us even when we don't love you in return,
> and neither life nor death,
>> nor angels nor principalities,
>> nor heights nor depths,
>> nor anything in creation
>>> can separate us from you.

We give thanks for your faithfulness,
so much more durable than our own.
You are the Father we always wanted,
we always needed.
We love you because you first loved us. Amen.

A sermon on the phrase "Our Father" from the Lord's Prayer ~ February 15, 2015

Sovereign King,
We approach your throne as subjects, not equals.
You are the king of all the nations and all people within the nations.
You are the kings of kings and lord of lords.
You are the alpha and the omega, the first and the last,
You always are, always have been, and always will be;
You are the Great I Am, not the great I was or the great I will be.
You are.

You have no predecessor, and there will be no successor.
We did not hire you and we can't fire you.
We didn't vote on you, we can't impeach you,
    and you're not going to resign.

We are your subjects, your slaves, your servants;
    You call and we answer,
    You send and we go,
    You commission and we serve,
    You initiate and we respond,
    You forgive and we are forgiven,
    You cleanse and we are made white as snow.

You are the great king of all the nations,
Others may claim to be king;
They flaunt their weapons and show off their hardware,
They intimidate the masses and crush their opponents.
But you, O Lord, sovereign king,
Come as servant in your power,
    And healer to the wounded,
    And giver to the needy,
    And helper to the helpless,
    And friend to the friendless.

We praise you today, among all the kings and presidents and governors
    and prime ministers, and executive leaders in this world.
You are our king and we bow down to worship you today.
In the name of Jesus, the king of glory, we pray. Amen.

        A sermon on the sovereignty of God ~ February 1, 2015

Almighty God,
We have many names for you, all intended to describe you in some way;
> Savior, Redeemer, Creator, Sustainer,
> Heavenly Father, Divine Comforter

The name we pass by is Judge.
It sounds so harsh, so 19th Century, so judgmental.
And our culture has determined that being judgmental is the worst sin.

We confess today we want to be judge over you, instead of being judged by you.
We want you to prove your existence.
We want you to defend yourself in light of evil, poverty, war, and injustice.
We want you to justify your activity in the world today.
We confess we want to judge whether or not you are worthy of worship, praise, and glory.
Forgive our adolescent arrogance and our tendency toward rebellion.

Father, give us a new and better understanding of your judgment,
> Like that of a father who loves his son,
>> One who wants that son to behave, respect others, especially the elderly,
>> One who wants that son to be diligent and not slack,
>> One who wants that son to chart a moral, upright path and stay away from the road of destruction.

You, Father want to show us genuine love by holding us personally accountable.

So teach us to number our days, to be active in doing good deeds,
To stay away from every kind of wickedness, evil greed, and depravity,
Envy, murder, strife, deceit, and malice,
Gossip, slander, insolence, arrogance, boastfulness,
Disobeying parents, senselessness, faithlessness, heartlessness, ruthlessness.
And lead us instead to goodness, righteousness, generosity, and servanthood.
Bless today the family of Jeri Philips who died yesterday at Forsyth Hospital.
Be very present to Ray Kight and his family as they prepare themselves to see Ann leave this world and enter the eternal home you have prepared for her.
Lead Kimi Crouch as she begins a new life in Christ.
Give her deep roots, strong faith, and a Christ-like spirit.
Be our judge, O God, so we don't have to carry that burden.
We bow before you in submission, and look up to you for hope.

In Jesus' name. Amen.

A sermon on "The Inevitability of Judgment" ~ 1 Kings 21 ~ January 11, 2015

*H*eavenly Father,
God of the Jews: God of Abraham, Isaac, and Jacob,
God of Sarah, Rachel, Esther, and Ruth.
You are the one who chooses,
> who elects,
> who establishes covenants,
> who marks a people as "your people."

We come today, most of us at least, as those who have now been
> grafted into the family of God,
> adopted as sons and daughters of Abraham,
> a part of the new Israel, called the church.

We believe in a Jewish Savior,
We read the letters of a Jewish missionary and consider them sacred.
We hold our Jewish spiritual kin close to our hearts.
And we are grateful for them for they have
> carried the promises of God,
> written and recorded the word we call Scripture,
> given us an inheritance that is rich and eternal.

Father, we also know you have called us to bear witness to
> this Jewish Savior, both to the Jew and Gentile.
You've called us to go into all the world and make disciples
> of all ethnic groups:
Jews and Gentiles, Africans and Americans, Europeans and Asians.

So strengthen us for the task, equip us for the call.
Sensitize us to the unique place of every group we will encounter.
Give us a love for each person we will meet.

Empower us with your Holy Spirit, so that we know
> when to speak
> and when to shut up,
> when to confront and when to retreat,
> when to offer a word of Scripture and when to offer a helping hand.
Do for us and through us what you have done throughout the ages:
> spreading your Word, healing sickness,
> filling backpacks for hungry children,
> making pillows and blankets for cancer patients.
We pray in the name of our Jewish Savior, Jesus Christ. Amen.

A sermon on "What Does the Gospel Mean to the Jews?" Romans 9-11 ~ October 19, 2014

*D*ear Daddy,
It's been a while since we've spoken to you, too long we know.
Life kind of got busy, we had other friends.
It was exciting to be with them, learn new things, experience new things.
We were going places and having a great time.
But along the way, we learned that good times don't last forever.
People can let you down.
We even let ourselves down.

Then we remember you,
In your recliner, always there, always available, always ready to help.
We remember your words of wisdom reminding us:
> Life is in giving more than receiving,
> Learn to be servants and you will find joy,
> Be compassionate toward all, especially the poor,
> Love your neighbor as yourself.

It wasn't as flashy as the Kardashians
But we've learned it's more true, more real, more trustworthy.

So, Daddy, I guess what we're saying is:
> We're sorry we ran off without telling you we were leaving,
> We're sorry we were so focused on ourselves when the world has such great need,
> We're sorry for taking you for granted, for not remembering the little things you taught us and the love you gave to us.

And we want to say thank you for loving us in the good times and bad,
For caring for us as infants and nurturing us with love,
Teaching us your commandments so that our days might be long
    on the earth,
And especially we want to thank you for sending your only begotten
    son, to die in our place.
We know we are the ones who deserved to die.
He didn't do anything wrong. We're the ones who did wrong.
But he died in our place. We know you sent him. We know he freely volunteered.
And by his stripes, we were healed, and adopted into your family.
So daddy, we just wanted to say, "Thank you. We love you.
We will never forget you.
From now on we are going to live like your sons and your daughters.
And we're going to try to carry on your work on this earth,
until we return to the homes you've prepared for us in heaven. Amen.

A sermon on Abba, Father ~ Romans 8:1-17 ~ October 12, 2014

*H*eavenly Father,
You know that most often I pray in concert with the sermon,
seeking your awakening to the truth we are proclaiming in word and song.
This week, however, I've been listening to a lot of people,
and have been struck by the loneliness of so many.

They are living with others but feel isolated and alone
    from those in the same home.
They have moved to a new city and feel shut out from all
    the friendships people already have with others.
They have started in a new school, and kids just don't pay attention
or care about the cliques they are in, which shut other people out.
They are in nursing homes, assisted living facilities, and places
where they miss their homes, their gardens, their familiar bed and chair.
They are in marriages which have the appearance of life,
    but are drowning in a sea of loneliness.

God, there is a place in your heart for the lonely,
    a place where we can go for friendship, intimacy, and real companionship.
Give that to our camp of lonely people.
Then lead us to be aware of others' loneliness.
Send us across the pew to reach out to the person we don't know.
Send us to the nursing home to hold the hand and listen to the
    voice of a lonely resident.
Send us to our spouse to give time and attention in ways they need.
Send us to our children, so they might know we care for them
    no matter how far they roam.
Use us to be your heart, your compassion, your friendship to
    a world starving for friendship.
In Jesus' name. Amen.

        After a long week of pastoral calls ~ October, 2014

𝒜lmighty God,
We come to you from a place of competing voices,
> competing gods,
> competing truths.
Our world, Your world, the one You created, is filled with proclaimers of good news.
Preachers with toothy grins and expensive suits
promise good news will come to us if:
> we will purchase the stock they are selling,
> adopt the diet they are hawking,
> live by the principles that guarantee happiness,
> move to a land overflowing with lush greens and crystal water.

We move from that world into this unusual community
proclaiming a different gospel, a gospel that is good news for:
> the oppressed and downtrodden,
> the rich and famous,
> the genius and the mentally disabled.

We are not ashamed of this gospel, this good news about Jesus.
We are not embarrassed to be his followers.
We are not inhibited to tell his story to all the world,
Because we believe it is the only eternally transformative story on record.
So, like Nolan Pegg, we put on the uniform of baptism to claim our identity.

As we pack this message in our travel bag and head into
> foreign countries,
> local neighborhoods,
> familiar homes,
> hostile work places,
We plead with you to give us simple clarity in our speaking this good news,
Announcing Jesus Christ as the Son of God,
> who died on the cross for the sins of the world
> and was resurrected from the dead by your unmatched power,
> so that all your promises find their fulfillment.

We ask that your Spirit go before us and prepare our way.
Make the crooked paths straight,
And the rough places smooth,
So that all will hear and know that,
Jesus Christ is Lord of All.
To the glory of the Father, in the name of the Son, through the power of the Spirit. Amen.

A sermon on "What is the Gospel?" ~ Romans 1:16-17 ~ August 17, 2014

𝒜lmighty God,
You are a God who is very demanding,
Commanding us to submit to you and no one else,
Requiring that we make no idols of money or fame,
Calling us to pick up our cross and follow Jesus.

In our zeal, we sometimes believe we are called
to make those demands and create new demands on others.
And so we creates laws,
We make rules,
We start traditions,
We make policies,
We write down regulations.
And these become our gods.
We worship, submit, and abide by these traditions of men,
And demand that others do the same.

Along this idolatrous path, we lose what's most important.
We begin to major on the minor issues,
And we confuse our rules with your commands.
We become sour, doleful, joyless people,
because there is no joy in keeping thousands of rules.
There's no mercy for ourselves or others who break the rules.
There's no love for the sinner and no gratitude for a loving God.

God, cleanse us today,
Of unrighteousness, yes,
Of sin, yes.
But also of our bent to righteous devotion to our laws,
And our demanding nature toward those who break our laws,
And our infatuation with arguments over intricacies, subtleties, and nuance.
Allow the witness of Hank Niblock's baptism
to remind us of the simple, obedient path that Jesus blazed for us:
obedience to the father, not to the rules of the sons.

Liberate us from our legalism.
Uncover our hypocrisy.
Lead us to the liberating path of the truth-telling man who said,
"Have mercy on me, oh God, for I am a sinner."
Have mercy on us, God, and lead us to have mercy on others.
In Jesus' name. Amen.

A sermon from Romans 2:1-16 ~ August 24, 2014

Don Gordon

*O*ur God, Our God,
    We remember the long day, covered by darkness,
when your Son and our Lord hung on the cross at Calvary.
The day was dark because evil seemed to be on the throne.
The day was dark because we could not see you at work.
We could only see your Son dying, crying out in lamentation.

And there are days we face that continue to be filled with darkness,
when we see our high school students learning how to escape bullets,
    instead of solving algebraic equations,
when we hold children dying of leukemia,
when we feel the deep pain of unexpected death in our families,
when terrorists escape and the innocent suffer.

We name this pain today.
We call it abandonment, loneliness, and depression.
We see the poor exploited and the powerful immune to their pathos.
We witness this and hear the taunts, "Where is your God?"

And so, we watch Jesus hang, and we wait.
We wait with longing, we wait in trepidation.
We wait, a heavy wait, edging to hope,
    not a frivolous, giddy hope,
But a heavy hope, grounded in sober, trusting waitfulness.

We wait through bullets and brain cancer, through isolation and abandonment.
We wait, sometimes beyond death.
We wait through the darkness, and we walk through the darkness toward you.
We wait for Friday to become Sunday.
We wait for resurrection to happen.
Trusting that you are in the darkness as well as the light.
Trusting you are in suffering, just as you are the source of joy.
Trusting that when you leave us, you will come back for us.
Trusting that you can and will redeem our suffering,
    through your relentless journey to love us through all eternity,
      and consummate your kingdom on earth as it is in heaven.
And so we utter in trust, "Into thy hands we commit our spirits."
In Jesus' name. Amen.

            A sermon on when Jesus leaves ~ John 14:1-14 ~ June 15, 2014

God sovereign and generous,
>   Who commands the rise and fall of the nations,
>   Who calls and has chosen many peoples,
>   Who creates life and controls the destiny of mankind,

And who, nevertheless, weeps when your children are harmed.
>   Who grieves over the rebellion of people,
>   Who suffers in death, more than we can imagine.

You are the one to whom we bring our lamentations.
We cry in your presence when we experience
>   The death of our mothers and fathers,
>   Our sons and daughters,
>   Our husbands and wives,
>   Our friends in wars.

We grieve at the loss of innocence,
>   Children abused and neglected.
We grieve over the loss of community,
>   Friends moved and gone,
>   Familiar spaces carved up and sold.

God, you comfort, you understand, you remain present to us.
You look with mercy on us as we crumple in helplessness.
You come to our aid, even when we are unaware of it.
You begin to heal us, and help us.

You stand before us an arsenal of hope.
You fight against the forces of despair and depression.
You bandage our wounds with the balm of Gilead.
You walk with us through the valley of the shadow of death.
When we fear evil, you take our hands, and promise:
I will never leave you, nor forsake you.

So today, we give you thanks for your intervention,
>   on our behalf in history,
>   at Ardmore, in North Carolina, in America, your world,
>   and those days still to come.
All praise to you, Life Giver, Comfort Maker, Hope Instiller.
In Jesus' name, we pray. Amen.

A sermon on grief ~ 1 Thessalonians 4:13-18 ~ May 25, 2014

*H*eavenly Father,
We confess you to be creator of heaven and earth.
We are dazzled by your power,
We are encircled by your mercy.
And now we come to this strange text we call Bible,
    with all its jots and tittles, all its laws and commands,
       all its stories and statistics, all its data and dictums.

We come with the expectation that you inhabit this text,
You live within it, speaking to us, calling us out or down.
In the English language, which Jesus never spoke, we hear you.
In letters and syllables Jesus never created, we feel him.
In the sound of preachers and readers of this text we hear Your Word.

We give thanks today that you have breathed life into this text.
We thank you for scribes, old and new, who have faithfully
    copied old stories or crafted oral stories so we might listen to them,
Telling us about
    Adam and Eve with serpents and fruit,
    Abraham and Sarah with toddlers running under their old feet,
    Jacob and angels wrestling through the night,
    Esther and Mordecai confronting kings and kingdoms,
    Paul and Barnabas traveling the world and preaching the gospel.

We give thanks for Psalm 23 and Psalm 46,
    which offer comfort to the families of
       Laverne McCard, whose brother's daughter-in-law died last week,
       and Amy Haire, who is recovering from surgery at Baptist Hospital,
       and Nancy Cleary, who is battling cancer with your strength.

We ask for your patience as we try to understand the stories and their meanings.
We ask for discernment and alertness so we'll know the truth when we read it.
We ask for freedom from old traditions that stifle meaning.
We ask for fidelity to ultimate truth so that we might be transformed by it.

We ask that we see what Jesus saw in these texts,
And that we live as Jesus did because of them.
In His name, we pray. Amen.

        A sermon on this strange book called "The Bible" ~ February 23, 2014

*A*lmighty God,
>We listen to the ancient poets who recorded your first words of our history, "Let there be light," and we are awed by the result.
>>Power from nothing,
>>Light from darkness,
>>Nuclear energy enough to cast the universe billions of miles from the origin.

Copernicus learned a little of your glory, but only a little.
Newton grasped a glimpse of your glory, but only a glimpse.
Einstein provided a calculation, but you supplied the energy.
Collins discovered the DNA sequence, but you stitched it together.
It was, however, your prophets who understood praise was the ultimate response to your awesome power.

We discover, you create.
We seek, you reveal.
We desire to know how you create, you desire that we know the Creator.
We are limited, you are unlimited.
We've been here for a few years, you are the Alpha and Omega.

And so at times we feel small, insignificant, of no account.
We wonder what our place is in this vast universe.
What are we, that you are so mindful of us?
What are we, that you should care for us?

And then we hear the ancient poet once more,
Assuring us we are the crown of your creation.
We are put in charge of this marvelous earth,
Caretakers and guardians.

And You, the One who creates 20-million galaxies,
Know the number of hairs on our head, and the sequence of our DNA.
You love us no matter how much or little hair we have,
No matter what kinds of defects are in our DNA,
No matter how much we understand you or love you back.

You love us like a parent loves her only daughter.

Listen to our praise, our songs directed toward your awesomeness,
From our childish lips comes forth praise.
The heavens declare your glory.
O Lord, our Lord, how majestic is your name in all the earth. Amen.

A sermon on the compatibility of science and faith ~ Psalm 8 ~ January 26, 2014

*H*eavenly Father,
Annmarie Grace Chancey was born Friday night
into the world and into our church family.
We have come here to celebrate her life.
Pete Peterson died this Wednesday,
leaving us for an unknown period of time.
We have come here to grieve our loss.
Sandra Talton is concluding 19 years of ministry of worship and music leadership.
We have come to thank you for your gifts to her that she has shared with us.
People seem to be coming and going all the time around here.
They walk with us, worship beside us, lead us, help raise our kids,
and then they are gone.
The world seems always to be changing.

In such a world, we return to the psalms and listen for your Word.
There is a city in the midst of this change, and it shall not be moved.
You are our city of refuge and stability,
You are our river whose streams make us glad.
You are the God of Jacob in our midst. And we will not be moved.

Today we are a people of many emotions:
    Grief in the presence of loss,
    Hope in the birth of new life,
    Thanksgiving for the rewards of retirement,
    Joy in the anticipation of new things.

We slow down and pause; we are still before you.
We acknowledge that you are God.
You are and will be exalted in the earth.
You are and will be confessed as author of life and death.
You are and will be the first and last, the alpha and omega.

We are your people, the sheep of your pasture,
the ones dear to you, the ones who depend on you
to lead us to the river whose streams make us glad.
In Jesus' name. Amen.

A sermon on worship in the midst of change ~ Mark 9:22-9 ~ August 25, 2013

*H*eavenly Father,
    The nights are sometimes too long and too dark.
Our knees have grown calloused, our faith has been pummeled,
Our prayers have hit the wall.
And we are speechless, wordless.
We, people of many words and easy phrases,
Do not know how we ought to pray.

Do we pray for miracles or acceptance?
    Recovery or endurance?
    Do we forgive or do we leave?
    A new job or adjustment to the current one?
We are stuck in our wordlessness and do not know how to pray.

And then you,
In the dark of night, in the flood of tears, in the agony of confusion,
Your Spirit intervenes with sighs too deep for words.
You bring us into communion with your holiness,
You pray on our behalf, you speak on our behalf,
You bring our sighs and groans before the throne of heaven;
    They will be heard.
There they meet your Son, already interceding on our behalf,
Before your throne of grace, God speaking to God,
All for us, your sons and your daughters.
You hear us when we can't hear You.
You take our prayers.
    Purify them,
    Distill them,
    Correct them.
They find a home, and your heart is glad.

And we can rest. We rest in your care.
So that even in our struggle to pray, we know you are praying for us,
    with us, through us, because of us.
Come, Holy Spirit, Come.
Rescue these prayers, transform them into a beautiful fragrance pleasing
    in your sight.
In the name of the Father, Son, and Holy Spirit. Amen.

    A sermon on the permissive will of God ~ 1 Samuel 8 ~ August 11, 2013

You God, are our true home.
In your presence, when we can finally be honest,
    we know we belong to you and not to this world,
    we know we are aliens and strangers on this earth.
Oh, there are times we feel at home in this world, when the family is together,
    when the food, the laughter, and conversations are old and familiar.
    these are the times and places that seem right. They seem like home.
But many times we find ourselves in unfamiliar places,
    the voices don't sound the same, the dialect is different,
    the food and weather are discordant, the land is strange,
    even the religion and the gods are alien.
And we feel a stab in the heart, a panicky doubt sets in about
    whether or not we belong,
    whether or not we will ever feel at home,
    whether or not we will ever experience the God of our youth.

Then you step in, into the places of our exile.
You call us to have peace,
    build homes, start families, get jobs, settle down.
In the middle of our strange places
    You call us to serve and worship You,
    the same God, the only God,
    the God of our beginning and the God of our destiny.
You remind us you are with us in these strange places,
    in places we'd rather not be,
    living as a widow or widower,
    as a divorced person,
    as one whose address is an assisted living facility,
    as one whose faith has been fractured by the frailties of man.

So help us sing again the familiar songs of Zion.
Let us worship with your people and hear the ancient commandments.
Let us see with eyes of faith your hand working in our lives,
    making a highway straight in the wilderness,
    raising up the valleys,
    making the hills low, and the rough places plain,
So Your Glory will be revealed, and we will see it with all people together.

And we will be home, with you, where we belong.
For the mouth of the Lord has spoken it. Amen.

        A sermon on living where you don't belong ~ Jeremiah 29 ~ July 28, 2013

*F*ather of Jesus,
You sent him to us, and we failed to recognize him.
You revealed yourself to us through him, and we were stunned.
You suffered in his body, and we turned away in shame.
You saved us through his death, and our lives are rebranded.

Today we exalt the name of Jesus, above all names,
For his healing deemed miraculous and normal,
For his beauty which can only be seen with a devoted heart,
For the revolutions he began for children offering them security,
And the ones he began for women offering them dignity,
For his brilliant mind made accessible to the weak-minded,
For his leadership that grows where men to do great things.

God, we recognize that Jesus is your gift to us,
But not only to us. He is your gift to the ages.
To children of Antioch,
The mothers of Corinth,
The senators from Rome,
The peasants of Nairobi,
The masses in New Delhi,
The powerful of Moscow,
The homeless of Detroit,
The students at universities.
He is your gift to us, and our gift to others.

So teach us to see him every day and love him every hour.
Forgive us when we neglect him, forget about him, and take him for granted,
For assuming he'll always be there for us when we need him,
But not feeling a like obligation to be there for him when he needs us.
Forgive us for using his name in vain and presuming upon his grace.
Bring us back into his care when we wander far away from him.

And let us sing praises with our heart, mind, soul, and strength,
Praising the name of Jesus, the Lamb of God,
> who takes away the sins of the world. In Jesus' name. Amen.

A sermon on the revolution Jesus started ~ Luke 2:41-52 ~ September 16, 2012

Almighty God,
Maker of heaven and earth, converter of chaos into order,
Creator of man and woman.
In your divine wisdom you have bestowed a gift upon every human.
Excepting Adam and Eve,
You have given each person a mother and father.
Until our recent tampering with your biosphere, there has always been a mother
And father for each child.
And how we need both.
Our mothers and fathers have been our teachers—
teaching us about commandments and cars and cooking.
They have been our nurturers—
preparing us for kindergarten and college and cloudy days.
They have been our rebukers—
revealing our wrong when no one else loved us enough to do it.
They have been our forgivers—
opening their arms after we have snubbed them, and opening their doors after we have
run away like a prodigal.
They have been our doctors—
reducing our fevers, prescribing medicines, staying nearby when we were throwing up.
Father, you have called us to honor them, respect them, remember them.
And so we do; At least we want to... but we need your help.
So help us honor them by living a life pleasing to God;
Let us honor them by speaking words of kindness and respect to them.
Help us to honor them in their old age by caring for them and nurturing their dignity.
Remind us of all they've done for us, and let us in turn give them reason to call their latter years blessed ones.
And when we fail, forgive us, help us to seek forgiveness and then forgive ourselves.
Give us, after our failures, a new day, a new life in relationships as you intended from the start.
Father, let us begin today, and leave this sanctuary with a new commitment of honoring our aging parents. Amen.

Sermon: "Honoring our Aging Parents" ~ March 18, 2012

Heavenly Father,
Over the past several weeks we have
experienced many earthly things:
> Vacations at the beach,
> Cooking dinner for the family,
> Washing clothes, paying taxes, getting the oil changed.
> Visiting our parents in the hospital,
> Applying to colleges and graduate schools.
> We've been doing normal stuff.

And so we return to this sacred place to read sacred texts,
to receive sacred counsel,
in order to live sacred lives.
But then we find you in these sacred texts calling us back to the world
of regular, mundane, sometimes scintillating tasks.
And we read in these texts about
> visiting people who are sick,
> paying our taxes,
> going to school,
> cooking meals,
> falling in love,
> marrying, living, and burying.

And we see you are active in the sacred,
while we are learning that all life is sacred.
It is a gift to be enjoyed, celebrated, and cherished.
So we celebrate the gifts of life,
falling in love,
going to school,
friendship in the neighborhood,
the thrill of seeing our children grow.
And we ask for grace and comfort associated with the risks of life,
broken hearts,
devastating divorces,
lonely nights for widows,
anxious days by the hospital bed,
car accidents in the dark of night.
Heal us from the wounds of life,
And lead us to live again, with all its risks,
even as you lived among us, with all its risks. In Jesus' name. Amen.

Sermon: "Straightening Out a Mess" ~ Titus 1:1-16 ~ April 29, 2012

*H*eavenly Father,
Who calls us into a world filled with injustice, saturated with poverty,
and lost in spiritual darkness.
Who calls the church into action, into prayer, into proclamation.
Who makes us the salt of the earth and the light of the world.

We thank you for the call to be salt, to be your agents in the world,
to bring zest and vitality to an otherwise dull world,
and to preserve all that is good, fresh, and holy from becoming
bad, rotten and unholy.
We thank you for the call of this church to be salt in Durham
and light for the RTP,*
for 134 years of salty preaching by pastors,
enlightened biblical guidance from dedicated teachers,
preserving work by faithful laymen and lay women,
and ministry scattered throughout our community—
> in the schools where children need to know they're loved,
> in the hospitals and clinics where the sick need healing,
> in the financial offices where people need wise counsel,
> in the big companies where employees need subtle, subversive grace.

We thank you for those who pray well and promote unity and think clearly and act with unusual grace. We thank you for the ministry to which you have called Yates Baptist Church.

Today, heavenly father, I want to thank you for my mother
who, for 80 years, has been a role model to her family and others
in the Christian way;
for being salt, little known outside her small circle,
for being light strong enough to reflect your glory even in her weakness.

May your Holy Spirit empower us to truly embrace our baptism
and the shared ministry of Jesus Christ;
that we may be salt that makes a difference
around the corner and around the world,
that we might be the light that dispels the darkness of evil
and the fear of the unknown.
Let our lives constantly and consistently point to you,
and not ourselves; to your power made perfect in our weakness.
Through Jesus Christ, the light of the world, we offer our prayer, Amen.

Sermon: "Subversive Grace" ~ Matthew 5:13-16
My mother, whose 80th birthday was this day, came from her nursing
home in another town to join our congregation for worship.

*Research Triangle Park

Almighty God,
In response to your grace,
>   let our first thoughts on this first day of the week be of you;
>   let our first impulse be to worship you,
>   let our first speech be Your name,
>   let our first action be to kneel before You in prayer.

Our response is effusive gratitude,
>   for your perfect wisdom and goodness,
>   for the love you have shown to us,
>   for the great and mysterious opportunity of life,
>   for the gift of the Holy Spirit in our lives.

We praise you and worship You, O Lord, in response to your grace.

Yet, when this worship service concludes, let us not forget your grace and think our worship is over and spend the rest of the day in forgetfulness of You.
Rather from this period of worship with your people, let your light and joy remain in us for the rest of the day and week,
>   keeping our thoughts holy,
>   keeping us temperate and truthful in speech,
>   keeping us faithful and diligent in our work,
>   keeping us humble in our estimations of ourselves,
>   keeping us honorable and generous in our dealings with others,
>   keeping us loyal to sacred memories of the past,
>   keeping us mindful of our eternal destiny with you.

On this day we thank you for the ministry of the Steiss family,
and seek your blessings for Danny, Johanna, and Marley as they get settled in Durham.
Give them friends they can enjoy, give them a church family that will love them,
and give them a sense of your guiding hand as they navigate new waters.
We also thank you for the ministry during the interim of Julia Johnson,
for her kindness to all, her diligence in her work, and her obvious commitment to Jesus.
Bless her and Kyle as they begin a new ministry at DMBC.
Father we also thank you for the gifts and ministry of the young voices of this choir,
for letting their praise become our praise to you.
Continue to gift them with voices of joy and hearts devoted to your Son, Jesus.
Receive all efforts of praise as an offering to You, the One who gives us life,
and gives it more abundantly than anything this world has to offer.
In Jesus' name, Amen.

Sermon: "Cheap Grace" ~ February 26, 2012
We celebrated the arrival of our new Minister of Students and
gave thanks to our interim minister and her future husband

Don Gordon

*H*eavenly Father,
We come today as debtors whose debts have been canceled.
Your Son came into a world of debt and paid it all.
We pray daily that you would forgive us our debts,
And we boldly qualify our prayer by the condition that
we would forgive our debtors.
We pray today for the cancellation of all our debts,
our sins, our greed, our lusts, our egocentric lifestyles,
And we pray for those who are in debt to us,
> who have sinned against us,
> snubbed us,
> lied about us,
> neglected us when we were in need,
> hurt our feelings,
> harmed our families.

And we offer forgiveness to them, as you have forgiven us.

We thank you that you have empowered us through your
grace to forgive, for we could not do it on our own.
It is you who has modeled debt retirement and reestablished
> new patterns of debits and credits.

You are the one who was rich and became Friday poor,
that being made poor, you would make many rich.

We are among those who are rich, forgiven of massive debt,
freedom from the bondage of our sins.
And we ask that you help us use our new found wealth
in a great pattern of redistribution,
Forgiving others, as you have forgiven us.
And so we pray as Jesus taught—

Our Father, who art in heaven, hallowed be thy name.
Thy kingdom come, thy will be done
On earth, as it is in heaven.
Give us this day, our daily bread.
And forgive us our trespasses, as we forgive those who trespass against us.
And lead us not into temptation, but deliver us from evil.
For thine is the kingdom and the power and the glory, forever. Amen

A sermon on forgiving ~ February 12, 2012

Our Good Shepherd,
We are a thirsty flock,
So you lead us to silent pools with refreshing water,
And we find life in them.

We search for green pastures and greener pastures,
And you bring us to grasses so rich and rare that
We are satisfied and our hunger abated forever.

We search for rest to end our weariness,
And you lead us to resting places and cool retreats,
Shielding us in the shadows of your grace.

We seek refuge from enemies on the outside
and enemies within,
And you build us a city of refuge
and deliver us from evil.

We come wounded and in need of healing,
And you anoint us with oil.
You serve us tea that comforts us,
And your love overflows.

Surely, your goodness and mercy surround us,
And we have found our true home
In your presence, the sheep in your flock,
And you will be our Good Shepherd forever and ever.
Amen.

A sermon on Jesus as a good shepherd ~ November 6, 2011

Don Gordon

Heavenly Father,
You are a God who calls and commands,
You send and you set forth;
> You called Sarah to go to another country,
> You called Esther to stand before a king and liberate her people,
> You called Deborah to judge your people,
> You called Mary to be the mother of the Son of God,
> You called Priscilla to teach,
> You called Miriam, Huldah, and four of Philip's daughters to preach.

God, we confess we don't understand your calling protocol;
We don't believe you call the right people—
You know, the rich and powerful, the strong and compelling,
Those that will automatically get a hearing.
You call men who stutter to speak for you.
You call women who are not supposed to speak to speak for you.
You call children to slay giants.
Your call to speak is so powerful that even if the called remained quiet,
> the rocks themselves would shout praises to your name.
Certainly, you don't need us to speak, but how can we remain silent
> when you do call.

Give us ears to hear your message proclaimed.
Give us hearts eager to heed your message.
Give us hands to lift up those who are called.
Give us feet to carry them when they are weak or wounded,
And give us a readiness and willingness to answer your call,
To go, to speak, to sacrifice, to forsake all for the sake of the Gospel
> and the glory of your name.

Stand by our beloved brothers and sisters in need of your presence this week.
Give Kim, Tripp, and Mikalah Shaw your daily bread.
Touch Amy Russell and her father and bring them healing.
Undergird LeAnne and Scott as they prepare to leave Durham
> and move to Waco.
Touch the widows who are lonely,
The mothers who fear for their children,
The fathers who don't have a friend they can turn to in crisis
And send us your grace to cover the multitude or our sins.
We pray this in Jesus' name. Amen.

A sermon on God's call ~ July 24, 2011

*H*eavenly Father,
We read stories in the Bible about thousands being fed with a few fish,
And people crossing safely through a sea to freedom,
Blind people receiving sight, lame walking, and the dead coming back to life.

And yet, O God, it doesn't seem that we can experience or see
these miracles in our world.
We do not always see the hungry get their food,
   or the thirsty receive a drink,
   or the frightened find a place of refuge and safety.
We live in a world where the stories don't always end
the way the stories do in the Bible.

And so we live in a world where doubt lives amidst our faith.
We want to believe. We say we believe. We stay because we believe.
But doubt tugs on our shirtsleeve and says, "Are you sure?"
We seek and search and pray and read and explore and travel in our mind.
We are searching for truth and certainty and unwavering security.
But it is elusive.
And we are driven back to you. Or maybe we're lured back to you.
Or perhaps it is you who comes to rescue us from our doubts.

You send us a Word that pierces our heart.
You send a Prophet who shows us the way.
You send us a Son who is the way, the truth, and the life.
And we are drawn to travel that way.
We are moved to acknowledge His truth.
We are compelled to model our lives after his life.
Therefore we come boldly, as he did, because he revealed your presence
   And security and blessing and peace.
In a world filled with hunger and thirst,
   fear and anger,
   hurt and violence, faith and doubt,
We pray for ourselves that we might be fed,
comforted and strengthened for our journey.
We pray that we might have enough faith to feed and comfort and strengthen and bless
or, as the Bible says,
enough faith to move a mountain.
We pray this in Jesus' name. Amen.

Sermon: "Faith and Doubt" ~ April 25, 2004

O God,
Your Spirit broods over the deep waters,
converting chaos into order,
raging waves of water into firm land and predictable waters.
You ignite worlds into being with your spoken Word,
And revival into churches with your preached Word,
And changed hearts with your living Word.

You are present with us today through your Holy Spirit,
    restoring broken lives,
    healing wounded bodies,
    teaching spiritual truths,
    forgiving reckless sins,
    empowering feeble wills.

Give us interpreters who can translate your speech
into a language we can understand.
Give us hearts that are receptive to your Spirit
so we can be changed into the likeness of your Son.
Give us wills that are soft and impressionable,
eager to do your will and follow your ways.

Move among us.
Blow mighty wind.
Breathe on us.
Shake the foundations of man-made fortresses.
Blast through our defenses.
We wait upon you, Holy Spirit.
We listen for your voice.
We sit still before you, Almighty God.
Holy Spirit, move in our hearts today. Amen.

                A sermon on the Holy Spirit ~ May 22, 2011

𝒜lmighty God,
We speak confidently of how all things are under your control;
    until we see cities charred with nuclear disasters,
    and tall buildings destroyed by terrorists,
    and children dying from leukemia.

And then we are baffled and bewildered,
    by terrorists who disturb our peace,
    by tsunamis that ruin our vacations,
    by death that reminds us of our mortality,
    by nuclear meltdowns that reveal the precarious nature of modernity.

Our confidence in modernity is a facade masking our fear.
And in our fear, we pray;
We pray to the point of blood, sweat, and tears.
    We ask that you protect your people,
    We seek healing for our friends,
    We solicit your forgiveness of our sins,
    We plead for you to right wrongs,
    and bring the schemers of injustice to their rightful end.

And we demand to be heard, we want a hearing;
    We want Japan to be healed of both its resistance to the Gospel
    and its collapsed infrastructure and nuclear meltdowns.
    We want Lela Garrett to come home from Duke Hospital.
    We want jobs for people, of all countries, who are willing to put in a day's
        labor to receive a decent day's wage.
    We want our children and grandchildren to profess faith in Christ,
        and live for Christ, and change the world for Christ.
    We want teachers in our schools to get through to hard-headed kids who
    are hell-bent toward destruction.
    We want goodness to trump evil, love to conquer hate, and we want to
    forgive others as you have forgiven us.
    And that's just part of what we want Lord, but we'll start there.

We wait on an answer Lord.
We know you will answer Lord, because you are the judge of all the earth, and
you are bound by your own holy instincts—
    for love, forgiveness, justice, and grace.
We pray in the name and power of your Son and our advocate,
Jesus the Messiah of Israel and Savior of the world.

      The Sunday after the Fukushima, Japan nuclear disaster ~ March 20, 2011

God of all truth,
We give you thanks for your faithful utterance of reality.
In your truthfulness you have called the world "very good."
In your truthfulness you have promised,
   "I have loved you with an everlasting love."
In your truthfulness you have assured us that Jesus is,
   "My beloved Son in whom I am well pleased."
In your truthfulness you have declared,
   "I am going to prepare a place for you."
In your truthfulness you have guaranteed that, "Nothing shall separate us
   from the love of God in Christ Jesus."

It is in your truth that we live and love,
And yet, we live in a world phony down deep,
   in which we participate with a wink.

Ours is a seduced world of half-truths and untruths,
     where good is called evil and evil is called good,
     where we exalt the proud and loud and scorn the meek and humble,
     where we applaud the young no matter what they do
        and dismiss the old no matter what they have done,
     where we take care of ourselves first and call that prudent
        and forsake those in need and call that reality,
     where we call war peace and peace war.
        so we rarely know when truth is being spoken.

Give us courage to depart the pretend world of euphemism,
    to call things by their right names,
    to love our neighbor as you love us,
    to give to others as you have given to us.
Overwhelm our fearful need to distort,
    that we may follow your path of truth-telling
    about ourselves and the world,
    that we may be tellers of truth and practitioners of truth,
We pray in the name of the One whom you have filled with "grace and truth."
Amen.

                A sermon on truthfulness ~ February 20, 2011

*H*eavenly Father,
We're taught in your Holy Word,
"Fear of the Lord is the beginning of wisdom."
Indeed you are the fountain of wisdom evidenced in the fact that you,
> created the world we live in and created us,
> know us better than we know ourselves,
> know our tomorrows while we can only guess at them, and
> know our neighbors, enemies, and friends just as well.

And you have made accessible more than a fair portion of your wisdom,
through your Word,
> the collective memory of your church,
> the teachers that have preceded us,
> and the daily presence of your living Spirit.

But we too often neglect your wisdom.
We trust in our own judgment more than yours.
We reason that we are the exception to the rule,
The rules don't apply to us.
We are busy and rationalize that we don't have time to consult you,
Or that we consulted you before and didn't get an answer.

Remove our folly.
Give us patience.
Plow the fields of our hearts preparing them for the slow growth of wisdom,
> the hard work of good judgment,
> the painstaking steps of prudence.

In this journey let us know more of you,
and in knowing you, ourselves as well.
We pray in the name of Jesus, the one who knows us fully,
> the one we yearn to know eternally. Amen.

Sermon: "How to Lose a Kingdom" ~ 1 Kings 12:1-17 ~ February 6, 2011

*H*eavenly Father,
We begin our prayer with confession:
Our sin has made the road from Jerusalem to Jericho a dangerous journey,
All our journeys from southwest Durham to northeast Durham are dangerous.
We dare travel many of these places at night, or in the daytime alone.
In these travels we have seen many suffering and in great need.
We have left them on the side of the road and gone to our own agendas.
We didn't know them so we passed them by.
We were in a hurry so we passed them by.
We were afraid someone would harm us so we passed them by.
We didn't like their race or their clothes or their origin,
    So we passed them by.

Forgive us for creating an atmosphere of danger rather than
nurturing your Garden of Eden.
Forgive us for passing by those in need instead of helping them.

In the midst of our confession we recognize that you send Samaritans
to help others and help us when we are the victims,
    to give us money when we are unable to pay our bills,
    to help when our cars on broken down on the interstate,
    to tutor us when our lessons are too difficult,
    to heal our wounds when we are bleeding and broken,
    to take us in when we are homeless or lonely or afraid.

We praise you, for in this broken world, you continue to restore
what has been broken,
You inspire the unlikeliest of humans to step up and help,
You bring people into our world we don't know, people who
have no reason to help us other than the instincts you implant
in their hearts.

So give us grateful hearts for all those Samaritans who have helped
us from infancy to the nursing home.
We praise you for all the good you inspire, all the evil you contain,
and the surprising grace you give to us.
Thank you for being on the road from Jerusalem to Jericho,
so we can see goodness responding to evil, and thus have a glimpse
of the kingdom of God on earth as it is in heaven.
In Jesus' name. Amen.

                A sermon on the Good Samaritan ~ November 7, 2010

*H*eavenly Father,
We come to you like a persistent widow.
We don't know where else to turn, who else to call on.
We know of no one else who can address our pleas:
> Our pleas for justice for the poor who can't afford high priced attorneys,
> Our pleas for food for children in India, Myanmar, and the Sudan,
> Our cries for mercy for Christians facing persecution in North Korea,
> Our petitions for our children who are being wooed by the secularists
>   and the libertines of our culture,
> Our questions about which path to follow next year or even tomorrow.

Listen to our prayers, hear our cries, grant us mercy, enact justice.
We wait for you to act;
Hear us pounding at the doors of your eternal throne.

And when we become tired of praying,
When we want to give up because the waiting was longer than we hoped,
When we no longer know what to say or how to ask,

Hold us up with your Spirit,
Pray for us and through us through your Spirit,
Give us words when we have none,
Give us wings like eagles so we can overcome our weariness,
Remind us that you listen, that you care, and you want us to persist
in our prayers.

And forgive us, when we stop praying,
Forgive us when we give up on you,
Forgive us when we decide we will move forward with or without you,
Forgive our foolishness, our impatience, our need to control you,
Forgive our demands that you act on our timetable instead of yours.

For you are our only hope,
You are the only water that is living,
You are the only bread that is eternal,
You are the only wine that is poured out for the forgiveness of our sin,
You are the only light that will never fade or grow dim.
So hear our thanks for being our hope and our eternal home. In Jesus' name.

A sermon on the persistent widow ~ October 10, 2010

Don Gordon

𝒜lmighty God,
We prattle on about the second coming of Jesus,
We use words like trumpets and rapture, sheep and goats.
So many in the history of the Christian movement have gone
so far as predicting dates and years of Jesus' return.
They embarrass us as they have embarrassed the Christian community.

Our greater perplexity is your delay—why you wait so long.
The delay is our problem more than the return,
For the delay means we must persevere,
We must wait with patience, we must hold on to the faith,
We must remain busy doing the work of the Lord until he says, "Time is up."

So God, we pray for those things: patience, endurance,
perseverance,and diligence in serving until the final whistle is blown,
and the scoreboard confirms the end has come.

In the meantime, we give you praise for new life, especially the
new life of Elliot Blake Norris born this week to Blake and Jennifer Norris.
We pray for Larry Mercer and his family as they grieve the death
of his mother;
We remember our former pastor Ray Hodge who stood by the grave
this week of his long-time wife, Joyce.
We lift up Kathleen Bishop before your presence, not that you are
unaware of her condition, but because we are aware of her condition
and know the time is short before she leaves us to be with you.

We confess today our negligence in tending to you.
We have gotten so busy with other people and things,
we have taken you for granted, thinking,
"Oh God will always be there when I return. No worries."
But the great threat about which we are so casual is that we
will never return, we will be so caught up in building our bank accounts,
or showcasing our lawns, or having fun that we put you on the back burner.
And with the years the back burner becomes farther and farther away
from the deepest desires of our heart.
So forgive us, God, for presuming upon you, presuming the door
is always open, the lights are always on, and the invitation is eternal. It's not.
So speak to us today and remind us,
the door will one day close,
the lights will be turned off,
and the invitation has an expiration date.
Give us ears to hear you today. Amen.

A sermon on the Parable of the Virgins ~ September 5, 2010

Almighty God,
You always have been, you always are, you always will be holy. Early in the morning our songs and dances shall rise to Thee. Merciful and mighty, compassionate and caring, forgiving and forgetting, you are holy. There is none like you in all the world, though many have tried and many claim to control others with the thought or words, "I am God." But you are the only God, the One God, revealing yourself as Father, Son, and Holy Spirit.

Your holiness compels us to adore thee. With our feeble hearts, our unholy minds, and our sinful lips we try to offer imperfect praise to your holiness, who deserves more. We long for the day when we can gather around your heavenly throne and bow before you and know you fully, even as you fully know us.

Holy God, we have prayed to you in recent days asking that you reveal the love of Christ through Jeanne Cross among the people of Nepal. We have asked that you work through Ryan Saunders, Sarah Gordon, Amy Saunders, and Katie Medlin in their camp work this summer, and you have answered our prayers. We asked that you accomplish your purposes through Winslow Carter and other missionaries from the YBA in Pennsylvania, and you did.

Father as we come to the end of a hot summer, lead us down the sure path of righteousness and obedience. Shield us from temptations to follow others gods, and give to us the strength we need each day to choose you over all others which seek to become our priorities.

Forgive us Holy One for our wrong choices:
    pampering ourselves while robbing you of your tithes and offerings,
    putting our needs for leisure and entertainment above your desire to
        commune with us in worship, prayer, and holy scripture,
    placing our family members above you, when it is you who created our
        families, and give them to us as a gift,
    placating our consciences by comparing ourselves to our culture
        rather than the life of Jesus.
We don't call these other allegiances gods, but we give them a higher priority than you.
Give to us a clean heart, O God, and renew a right spirit within us. Renew within us a commitment to the covenant relationship with you.

Almighty God, you are holy. We join all creation, all that you made in praising your name. Holy God, God in 3 persons, blessed Trinity. We bow before your holiness, in the name of the Father, Son and Holy Spirit, Amen.

A sermon on our Trinitarian God ~ August 8, 2010

*H*eavenly Father,
The world can be a hard place,
Those who believe in your Son are a minority,
though that minority status is sometimes camouflaged
in the Bible belt of the U.S.
We are lured by the Tempter to seek power through
the world's eyes: money, status, strength of arms.
We are inundated by detractors and cynics who call us
naïve, gullible, and desperate.

And yet we hear your voice, feel your presence, and
see your power in your church and your Word.
We hear your words of assurance, reminding us that
>we are yours,
>
>we have eternal life with you,
>
>we have hope no matter what our circumstances,
>
>we have power even while imprisoned,
>
>we are your sons and daughters and always will be.

Today we ask that you drown out the other voices,
>voices of
>
>confusion,
>
>doubt,
>
>despair,
>
>fear,
>
>uncertainty.

Replace them with your words of
>assurance,
>
>confidence,
>
>resolve,
>
>perseverance,
>
>comfort,
>
>and love.

Lead us to be people of confidence,
> not in our own abilities or goodness,

But in your faithfulness and fidelity to your covenant
> and your gift of grace in Jesus Christ our Lord.

Give us assurance of eternal life through Jesus Christ
> your Son and our Savior,

In whose name we pray, Amen.

A sermon on the assurance of eternal life ~ July 7, 2010

Advent

Almighty God,
We magnify your name, our soul glorifies you.
Our spirit rejoices in you, our Savior.
We are so joyful that you have been mindful of us,
that you remember your servants.
We rejoice in the gift of your Son, born of a virgin,
    the One called Immanuel,
        God with us.
We rejoice in the community we call church,
the Bible we call your Word,
the Spirit that empowers us to see the unseen.
We can hardly give utterance to our praise.

And then we gripe and complain.
We lament and sorrow.
We sometimes worship you as if you were the tax collector
rather than Savior.
We sleep when we should sing;
We frown when we should smile;
We slouch when we should dance.
We confess our joylessness to you today, O God,
And ask that you replenish us,
Surprise us with your joy.

Then we will go to Helen Gaspard in the hospital with
the good news that Jesus heals.
We will come to sleep on the church floor with our
homeless guests and tell them the good news of the poor finding homes.
We will tell our neighbors there is a Savior greater than
the fragile souls who run the government.
We will go to Haiti with joy,
    to India with ecstasy,
    to the public schools with glad hearts,
    to our homes with a song in our voices.

You, O God, giving birth to miracles in stables and states.
Do a miracle among us, through us, beyond us.
And we will watch and wait and wonder and give ourselves to you completely.
Amen.

A sermon on Mary's Magnificat ~ November 27, 2011

*H*eavenly Father,
We don't need Wikileaks to know there are dirty little secrets
behind guns and power.
There are Herods who roam the earth bent on violence,
>   Paranoid they will lose their grip on power,
>   Willing to destroy others who threaten their future,
>   Casting a dark spell over your good creation.

Into this dark world you come, a world filled with violence and vengeance,
a world full of devils, evils, and the slaughtering of the innocents.
You have come to be with us, here in our Bethlehem,
where innocent children die of guns, malaria, and abortions.
You have come to be with us in our Egypts, where refugees come
from Afghanistan, Iraq, and Syria.
You have traveled with us to Nazareth because our
hometowns are too dangerous.
You come with your light to cast out darkness.

In this Christmas season,
>   when toddlers are threatened in Haiti from the disease of cholrea,
>   and innocents in churches are gunned down in Iraq,
>   and children are suffering with cancer at Baptist Hospital,
>   come to us again.
Bring your light into our dark world.
Enlist us in your mission to protect the children, defend the innocent,
and love the forgotten.
Send us as your candles into the wind,
Empowering us with the Spirit of your Son
so our candles will never fade in the sunset
when the rains set in.
Take us, your baptized sons and daughters, and send us on
your mission to rescue the refugees from starvation and deprivation.
Shine your light in us and through us in this dark world. Amen.

A sermon on Herod ~ December 14, 2014

O God, you have texted us again.
We just pulled it up and read it from our iBibles.
This Isaiah guy sounds a little crazy:
>—wildernesses rejoicing and blossoming;
>—eyes of the blind opened;
>—ears of the deaf unstopped;
>—lame leaping like deer;
>—and streams in the desert.

I guess he hasn't heard about global warming and deserts expanding,
and the weather producing fewer blossoms for more people.
I guess he hasn't known about death and disease we face.
We just learned that Ruby Hill died last night, and we're sad.
We know that Barbara Crocker and Kathy Barron are still
recovering from surgery.
We know there are dear friends in our church with cancer.
Lord, what about those people?
When will they leap like a deer and see blossoms in the desert?

Your texts keep coming:
"It will be called the Way of Holiness.
The unclean will not journey on it;
it will be for those who walk in the Way...
They will enter Zion singing; everlasting joy will crown their heads."

God, I suppose this text is for those in the deserts as well,
For Ruby's family, reminding them of Ruby's entrance to Zion,
For Kathy and Barbara, reminding them that ferocious beasts
of illness, infection, and isolation will be kept off the highway,
And those with cancer will not walk alone in this land
> where every valley will be exalted
> and every mountain made low,
> the crooked straight
> and the rough places plain
> and the glory of the Lord will be revealed
> and all flesh will see it together
> for the mouth of the Lord has spoken it.
And so it is, and so it will be,
This is the highway we will walk forever. Amen.

Sermon: Streams in the Desert ~ Isaiah 35:1-10 ~ December 18, 2011

*H*eavenly Father,
We are a fearful people, and we dwell in the midst of a fearful people.
Fearful of our world falling into the hands of rogues and terrorists,
Fearful of moral decay undermining our nation and our future,
Fearful of too many dangers, toils, and snares.
Fearful of not doing well,
of being found out,
of being left out,
of being abandoned,
of growing old.
And then we hear, astonishingly in the midst of our fearfulness,
an angel, your messenger, a voice say, "Fear Not!"
Do not be afraid, God has come to earth, He appears through the virgin birth.
Emmanuel, God is with us.
With us in wealth and poverty,
With us in success and failure,
With us for better or worse.
We come tonight to hear these words and experience their reality.
We come to be changed, to be made new, to overcome our fears.

So speak to us through these voices, these messengers from God, these singers who walk in our world and still say, "Fear Not."
Because these words come from you, O Father, we will not fear.
Though the earth should change,
though the mountains shake in the heart of the sea.

For whom shall we fear with you as our light, our strength, our hope.
You bring good tidings of great joy.
Unto is born a king, in the city of David, a Savior has been born.
He is Christ the Lord.
And now our fear is met by the stronger force of praise and thanksgiving.
Glory to God in the highest, and on earth, peace, good will toward all people.

Receive now our worship, cover our fear, and accept our hearts of praise,
In the name of the one lying in a manger, Jesus Christ our Lord. Amen.

    Opening prayer for the Christmas Cantata "Fear Not" ~ December 2003

Don Gordon

*H*eavenly Father,
More than any other day of the year,
this Sunday corresponding with Christmas Day we are aware you are a giving God.
You the Creator, giver of goodness, creator of all that is,
    you faithfully provide for us.
You our Redeemer, giver of new creation,
    you graciously give us a redeemer.
We are children of your provision,
    daughters and sons of lavish provision.
We live amidst ample food, ample clothes,
    ample housing, ample cars, ample stereos,
    ample friends, ample security,
We have ample and count on it,
and we reckon our luxuries to be necessities.
Today we express our gratitude for your provision.

In this season of peace, we notice the war refugees in Iraq,
We notice the children with AIDS in Nairobi,
We notice there are still homeless families in Durham,
We notice that Mary Taylor had a fall and is spending Christmas
    Day at the Hillcrest Center,
We notice, amidst all the lights of Christmas, the darkness
and uncertainty faced by people.

And our notice turns our hearts and eyes back to you,
    The giver who speaks out on behalf of the refugee,
    The giver who provides hope and help for the homeless,
    The giver who provides miracles for some and love for all,
    The giver who provides a Savior in a manger and a cross.

We know wise men still seek you and bring you gifts.
We follow the magi to Bethlehem,
And we are compelled to bring you gifts,
And give gifts in your name,
So that we, driven by your generosity, might become generous people.

Today,
For all your gifts, for all your provisions, for all your generosity,
we stand to give you thanks.
We thank you in the name of the loveliest of names—Jesus—
    The child born to us, the Son given to us.
    Wonderful Counselor, Mighty God, Everlasting Father, Prince of Peace. Amen.

Christmas Day ~ 2011

Holy Week

O God,
The drumbeat of our sin echoes in the church this holy week.
We reflect on the events this coming dark Thursday with its
betrayal, denial, abandonment.
We see this Friday in the distance, throwing our language on its head.
We call it good, and we see nails, thorns, torn flesh, and death.
We listen to the drums of ancient truth:
> "Despised and rejected by men,
> A man of sorrows,
> Acquainted with grief,
> No one is righteous, no not one
> All have sinned and fallen short of the glory of God."

We ponder the atrocious evils in the world:
Hitler, Stalin, Hussein, Bin Laden,
While we hope to avoid listening to the tape of our own lives.
Such ordinary sin:
> subtle greed,
> simmering anger,
> perpetual apathy,
> work with no Sabbath,
> love with no commitment,
> religion without heart.

The cadences of our sin are not extraordinary like a rock-n-roll drummer,
But more like the bass drum of a symphony—
Methodical, steady, perpetual, and underneath all the sound and fury of our lives.
It doesn't stop, at least not for long.

During this Holy Week, bring honest reflection and confession front and center.
Plant our wobbly knees in front of the cross all week long.
Bring us to gaze upon the daunting image of your Son,
so sinless, so self-giving, so loving, so holy,
And hold us to the uncomfortable stance of presenting our sins before Him.
Don't let us leave, walk away, and avoid honest self-awareness.
Don't let us shut our eyes and neglect His suffering for our sins.
Don't let us go on as if this is an ordinary week,
With our sins casually floating around like white clouds on a spring day.

Move us to stand at the foot of the cross,
So that we might see his oppression and affliction,
So we might touch his trembling hands and see the forsakenness of his eyes.
Move our hearts to see the punishment that brings us peace,
And see the wounds that bring our healing.

As we stand before the cross, we speak words in harmony with the ancients, "Thank you Father, for the Lamb of God who comes to take away the sin in our world." Amen.

Palm Sunday ~ April 1, 2012

𝒜lmighty God,
We speak confidently about your sovereignty, your power,
Of how all things are under your control;
Until we see cities swept away by tsunamis,
And tall buildings destroyed by terrorists,
And children dying from leukemia.

Then we are drawn up short;
by terror that strikes us in our privilege,
by violence that shatters our illusions of well-being,
by death that reminds us of our at-risk mortality,
by smoke and fire that have the smell of humanity.

We are bewildered, knocked off stride, and frightened,
And in our fear, we pray.
We pray to the point of blood, sweat, and tears.
>We ask that you protect your people,
>We seek healing for our friends,
>We solicit your forgiveness of our sins,
>We plead for you to right wrongs, and
>bring the schemers of injustice to their rightful end.

And we demand to be heard, we want a hearing.
>We want Haiti to be healed of its resistance to the gospel and its poverty.
>We want Sandy Cleary to be healed of cancer.
>We want jobs for people—of all countries—with a decent enough wage to live on.
>We want our children and grandchildren to profess faith in Christ, and live for Christ and change the world for Christ.
>We want teachers in our schools to get through to hard-headed kids who are hell-bent toward destruction.
>We want goodness to trump evil, love to conquer hate, and forgiveness for ourselves and our enemies.
>And that's just part of what we want Lord, but we'll start there.

We wait on an answer, Lord.
We know you will answer Lord.
Yet, not our will, but thy will be done.
In the name of Jesus we pray, Amen.

A sermon on Jesus' Gethsemane prayer ~ March 6, 2014

*H*eavenly Father,
We watch from a distance this week as your Son enters his trials.
We shrink in the presence of dark treachery unfurled on the earth:
> false accusations,
> undeserved cruelty,
> relentless taunting,
> agonizing aloneness.

We hear the measured, thoughtful, profound words of our Lord
> in the face of this onslaught of accusations.
We hear him speak of his kingdom and power,
> yet not using that power to overthrow his accusers.
And we hear his silent witness, like a lamb led to slaughter,
> like a sheep before his shearers, he opens not his mouth.
His words and his silence stand as beacons of light
> in the midst of darkness
They are testaments of truth in a courtroom saturated in falsehood.

We are in awe before this man,
We are knocked to our knees by his faithfulness,
We are humbled by his willingness to absorb this evil
> and take our sins upon himself.

We confess our complicity in this darkness,
for it was not just Pilate or Herod or the Jewish leaders
that sent Jesus to the cross.
It was for our sins that he was chastised,
and it is by his stripes we are healed.

Move our hearts today to feel his passion.
Give us eyes to see his suffering.
Plant within us the convictional truth that all of this
human treachery, blatant evil, and grave injustice is
met with perfect love for our sakes.

As we stand before the cross, we speak words in harmony with the ancients,
"Thank you Father, for the Lamb of God, who comes to take away the
sin in our world." Amen.

A Sermon on the Last 24 Hours of Jesus' Life ~ April 10, 2011

O God,
You are the faithful one,
Fulfiller of promises,
Steadfast when the days are sunny,
Offering a rock upon which to stand when the storms of life come.

You do not waiver in your love for us,
You do not abandon us at the first sign of trouble,
You do not leave us when we forsake you.

But we, O God, have something to confess today.
We need to come clean, lest our guilt lead to despair
    and despair lead to suicide.
We have betrayed you.
Yes, we thought you would rescue us from pain,
And when we felt pain nevertheless, we chose another deity.
Yes, we got tired of doing right, loving mercy, acting for justice,
So we joined the masses wearing their cloaks of self-protection
    and carrying their clubs of retaliation.
Yes, we were confronted with a decision to stand up for you
    when we knew it would cost us dearly,
And we loved the privilege and prestige and profit coming from betrayal.
Yes, we needed those 30 silver coins.

Oh, God who is faithful through all eternity,
We confess,
    we have more of Judas's blood in us than we want anyone to know,
including you.
But we can't carry this guilt any longer.
The 30 pieces of silver in our pocket are going to cause us to drown
before we cross the Jordan.
We must snatch this betrayal back from Satan, who is salivating over it,
and give it to you so you can arrest it in its tracks,
nail it to a cross, kill it, bury it, and lay it in a tomb,
So that we can live again, rejoice again, dance again
and experience the resurrection of life in the Kingdom of God.
This is our prayer, and we know you will be faithful with it. Amen

A sermon on Judas's betrayal ~ March 23, 2014

Loving God,
We are surrounded by those who deny you:
> Atheists who don't believe,
> Agnostics who aren't sure,
> Powerful people in North Korea and Saudia Arabia
> threatened by the Christian faith.

But then there's us:
> Your people,
> People who worship you in pews on Sundays,
>> but find it inconvenient to follow you on Friday nights,
>
> People who sing of our faith, but lose our voices
>> when our peers sing a different song.

Today, we dare look at Jesus once again, and hear the cadences of his suffering,
> despised and rejected by men,
> a man of sorrows, and familiar with suffering,
> stricken by God,
> pierced for our transgressions,
> crushed for our iniquities.

And we are dazzled by the extravagance of his suffering love,
> like a lamb led to slaughter,
> as a sheep before his shearers,
> a divine, inscrutable will to crush him.

We are staggered by such love,
Love uncoerced, given freely and voluntarily,
Suffering embraced, not shunned.

You have moved purposefully toward the cross,
So we might be moved redemptively toward your kingdom.
By your stripes we are healed.
Our denials are covered with your grace and forgiveness.
You redeem us when we don't deserve it.
Grateful is an understatement for how we are toward you.
And we intend to live our lives as a testimony to you. Amen.

A sermon on Peter's denial ~ March 30, 2014

*O*ur God, Our God,
We remember the long day covered by darkness
when your Son and our Lord hung on the cross at Calvary.
The day was dark because evil seemed to be on the throne,
The day was dark because we could not see you at work,
We could only see your Son dying, crying out in lamentation.

And there are days we face that continue to be filled with darkness,
> when we see our high school students learning how to escape bullets
>> instead of solving algebraic equations,
> when we hold children dying of leukemia,
> when feel the deep pain of unexpected death in our families,
> when terrorists escape and the innocent suffer.

We name this pain today. We call it abandonment, loneliness, and depression.
We see the poor exploited, and the powerful immune to their pathos.
We witness this and hear the taunts, "Where is your God?"

And so, we watch Jesus hang, and we wait;
We wait with longing, we wait in trepidation;
We wait, a heavy wait edging to hope,
Not a frivolous, giddy hope
But a heavy hope, grounded in sober, trusting waitfulness.

We wait through bullets and brain cancer, through isolation and abandonment.
We wait, sometimes beyond death.
We wait through the darkness, and walk through the darkness toward you.
We wait for Friday to become Sunday.
We wait for resurrection to happen,
> Trusting that you are in the darkness as well as the light.
> Trusting that you are in suffering, just as you are the source of joy.
> Trusting that when you leave us, you will come back for us.
> Trusting that you can and will redeem our suffering
>> through your relentless journey to love us through all eternity
>> and consummate your kingdom on earth as it is in heaven.

And so we utter in trust, "Into thy hands we commit our spirits."
In Jesus' name. Amen.

A Good Friday Prayer ~ 2011

O God,
We watch and listen as Mary and Joanna and others take spices to the tomb,
We walk with them, some of us, at least;
As they take their disappointment to the grave,
    their lingering, but weary love,
       their dashed hopes and pummeled faith.
Others of us have gone on with our lives,
    back to work to make a living,
    outside to play to enjoy the spring air,
    wandering around in our minds for some place to land.
We come to the tomb, the place they laid Jesus,
    and he is not there!
    He is risen!
    And we are stunned!
    Our bewilderment overflows,
    Our categories are shot down,
    Our world views are confronted with your Presence.
We drop to our knees to worship you,
  We want to touch you, like Thomas, to know you're real,
  We want to touch you, like Mary, because we love you,
  We want to sit with you and talk, because we need forgiveness like Peter,
  We want to break bread with you, like Cleopas, and hear you explain
  the Bible in light of this resurrection.
  We want all of this, Lord.
We want it all.
Give yourself to us, O Lord,
    So that we might go and tell the others,
    the used to be disciples who have given up,
    the ones who never heard of you and will be amazed,
    the ones who are stumbling through life with no vision, no hope, no dream.
Easter us, God.*
Resurrect our faith, Jesus.
Bring peace.
Break injustice down and resurrect justice.
Easter us, God.
And hear our stunned, amazed, grateful thankfulness,
And our songs of Hallelujah!
Christ is risen. He is risen, indeed!
Amen!

        * Walter Brueggemann is the first person I heard use the word "Easter" as a verb.

World Communion Day

God of the East,
We pray for our brother and sisters in the Middle East facing violence.
Protect families standing in the way of the onslaught of ISIS.
Give refuge to Muslims, Christians, and Jews who are targets of
terrorism and murder.
As we direct our eyes toward India, strengthen the IBTS and other
Christian gatherings planting churches, making disciples, and
staffing orphanages.
For China, God, we ask that you strengthen the churches—the official
churches and unofficial ones—that are grounded in Jesus Christ.
We pray for boldness in the declaration of the gospel for those
on the Mainland, as well as Taiwan and Hong Kong.

God of the North,
We pray for our brother and sisters in Russia, Scandanavia, Greenland
We ask that you strengthen the churches of Jesus Christ that
are Orthodox and the free evangelical churches.
Let the Word of God continue to spread in these cold regions,
may the fire of your Holy Spirit invade this land with truth, love, and
reconciliation.
Give the people hope when they feel despair,
and connect them to your people around the world in koinonia.

God of the West,
We pray for our brothers and sisters in Europe,
where so many churches have lost their vibrancy and relevancy.
Start a new thing in your church that would capture the heart of the young.
Moving west from Europe, we pray for churches in America,
Calling our churches to raise a prophetic voice against consumerism
and the assumption that we can spend our way out of problems.
Give our leaders the instinct to help the people more than helping themselves,
And empower our churches to be agents of moral and spiritual influence
in this land of diversity.

God of the South,
We pray for our brothers and sisters in Africa,
We ask that you help them use their land well to feed the people.
Give nations under duress from religious strife, spaces for
peace and freedom.
Protect this continent from further spread of the Ebola virus,
and heal those who have already contracted this disease.
In South America, God, we pray that you would strengthen your church.
Empower evangelists to spread the Gospel,
Take the reawakened churches in Brazil and Argentina and scatter

them into villages throughout Bolivia, Peru, and Columbia.

O God, bring peace to the four corners of the earth
And lead us to righteousness in our own land.
Bring salvation to all the nations,
Make us instruments of your peace,
Bring the Gospel of Jesus Christ to our communities,
our nation, and our world. Amen.

Prayer for World Communion Day ~ October 4, 2014
(our people physically faced the 4 corners of the earth as we prayed)

All Saints' Day

Pastoral Prayer

God of our mothers and fathers long gone and treasured,
God of our friends and mentors short-lived but long remembered,
God of our grandchildren, yet to be, but awaited,
> Our lives are deeply rooted in miracles before us,
> Miracles of birth, caring, loving, and granting mercy.
> Our faith is richly set in the lives and faith of the old saints.
> We acknowledge them too seldom, just as we do with you,
> Our vocation is shaped by all those who have risked for your purposes,
> and worked for your kingdom:
>> keeping the nursery,
>> teaching the Bible,
>> showing kindness,
>> praying for the sick,
>> helping us sing.

And now, remembering the saints returned to glory in 2010,
> we are made mindful of our own place and call,
> and our own time of obedience.

We pray that you would find us faithful and persevering to the finish line
> of this great race of holy living,
>> surrounded by such a great cloud of witnesses.

We pray for ourselves and for your whole church,
> a willingness to serve in unknown and obscure places,
> a readiness to risk comfort and pleasure for faith and service,
> a steadiness in the face of opposition and even persecution,
> a steadfastness to confront and expose our own sins and run from them.

This day we particularly pray for the people of Haiti combating cholera.
We pray those who thirst may receive water, those who hunger, food;
We pray for shelter for those wandering around crumbled homes;
We pray that the Christian community of the world will incarnate the
> love of Christ for this people, and a new day will dawn out of the darkness.

We also pray for the family of Patty Watson as they mourn her death last week,
as we do the family of Lamar Willis whose mother died Friday evening.
Touch these families with your grace and comfort them with your Spirit.

We end our prayer with utter gratitude for this great cloud of witnesses,
And most especially for Jesus Christ, the author and perfecter of our faith,
who for the joy set before him endured the cross, scorning its shame.
In him, and because of him, we do pray. Amen.

All Saints Day ~ 2009

Baptism

Almighty God,
Hidden from us in many ways, we confess you through ritual;
We confess you in actions that are repetitive and sacred,
We baptize in waters that are ordinary but holy,
We eat bread and drink the fruit of the vine that is bitter but sacred,
We sing songs, hymns, and psalms that declare your glories,
We hear your written word alive with your vibrant breath,
We hold hands declaring unity in a fractured world.

We do not see you, but we dare to let others see our faith in you,
So we declare you make us new creations in our baptism.
We announce that Macey Creech is your beloved child
and that you are pleased with her.
We name your divine activities in history through contemporary songs,
We listen for your distinctive voice through the reading of Holy texts,
We act our faith out, because you have acted in faithfulness,
We perform for you in response to your performance in our lives.

But we make a public confession today as well,
That we act out of habit instead of sacred memory,
Singing words that are on the page but not our hearts,
Witnessing a baptism, but not living as those baptized,
Eating bread, drinking wine, but not living in Christ.
Hearing only words and not Word of God, not Word from God.
Holy God, we act without memory, passion, and flagrant love.

So turn our rituals from forgettable habits to holy moments
    bursting with your presence,
    dripping with passion,
    connecting our heart to yours,
    moving from earth to heaven in one bound.
Make our rituals of singing, baptizing, eating, reading, touching
    infused with your grace,
    grounded in your holy presence,
    empowered by your Spirit,
    and filled with life-changing energy.
Make the ordinary sacred and the sacred accessible
To us, your people, your sons and daughters, your ambassadors
To the world at large.
In the name of your greatest act,
    The incarnate Word of God, Jesus Christ our Lord. Amen.

June 13, 2010

Missions

*H*eavenly Father,
You called an old man, Abraham, and he went to an unknown land.
You called an aging Sarah, and she laughed.
You called a fugitive, Moses, and he resisted and talked back.
You called charming Esther to speak up for your people;
    she cleared her throat and proclaimed your message.
You called Matthew to put away his accounting books,
        and Luke to put away his stethoscope,
        and Saul to put away his prejudice and hate.
And you call us.
    You call us to carry the Gospel into a violent world,
        to pray for those who go where we can't,
        to teach the young about the hungry and hurting people.
    You call women and men, young and old,
            single and married,
            rich and poor,
            Lumbee Indians and Scottish mountaineers,
            brimming with confidence and overwhelmed with insecurities;
        to surrender our all for you,
        to sacrifice our daily comforts for a world that is lost,
        and to serve Jesus Christ with all our hearts,
            with every emotion,
            with all our intelligence,
            with every ounce of our energy.
This weekend, we are here to listen to your call,
        to lay at your feet our fears, frailties, and phobias,
        giving them to you,
        and awaiting your demanding call and extravagant love.
Speak Lord, for we are listening. We are all in for you,
        because there is no other that deserves our all,
        there is no other that can redeem us,
        there is no other that can make us beautiful, holy, and pure.
In the extravagant name of Jesus we pray, Amen.

Opening prayer for the Annual Gathering of the WMU of North Carolina
whose theme for the event was "Extravagant Love" ~ April, 2015

*H*eavenly Father,
It is not for us to know when the world will end, or
How the dead are resurrected, or
How your Son was both fully human and fully God.

But we have a story,
    a story about a Savior,
    a story about how You entered the world in order to bring forgiveness,
    redemption, and reconciliation to all humanity,
    a story we are called, compelled, and commissioned to share.

We are grateful that you continue to call missionaries who leave their homes and countries to tell this story. We pray for them as they travel and then live in places like Jordan; Southeast Asia; Miami; Dearborn, Michigan (Arabs); and New York (United Nations) to tell this same story. And we ask for your grace and protection on them as they learn and speak new languages,
    deal with cultural differences,
    customs that are strange,
    and food that seems odd.
Protect our missionaries from harm from oppressive governments
    and suspicious local leaders.
Give them boldness to share the Gospel and wisdom to know when
    they should be silent.
Surround their children with friends so they can have what we all need—what we all want—a community of people with whom we can laugh and play, learn and grow, cry and receive comfort.
    Give them enough victories in their work to feel affirmed in their call, and
        give them perseverance in their defeats so they will put their dependence
        on you.

Father, we also pray that you would kindle the fires of missions within us:
    rage within us,
    convert this rage to word and deed,
    spread your story through our stories,
    send us on mission,
    light us up, send us out, and bear fruit for your gospel.
In Jesus' name, Amen.

        A service supporting missionaries ~ February 10, 2013

O God,
Long ago a young virgin said "Yes" to your strange request.
Your initiative and her faithful response began a cyclone of miracles.
This miracle became Incarnation, Redemption, Salvation, and Resurrection.

In this season of calling for peace, we are grateful troops are returning from Iraq.
We pound on the gates of heaven, calling for peace on earth and goodwill toward men.
>   Let violence be replaced by respect.
>   Let fear be overcome by love.
>   Let distrust transform into trusting partnerships.
>   Let there be peace on earth,
>   in Bagdad and Nasiriyah,
>   in Tehran and Damascus,
>   in Bethlehem and Jerusalem.

Father, lead us to be people like Mary, to say "Yes" to you even
>   when it doesn't make sense,
>   when it seems your call is impossible,
>   when following you requires risk, pain, and sacrifice,
>   when following you means we might have to endure ridicule and scorn.
Lead us to say "Yes" to your claim on our lives.

Father, we ask today that you touch Kathy Barron, who is sick and in the hospital.
We thank you for the healing of Judy Mykelbust, who left the hospital this past week and is recovering from surgery at home. We thank you for being present with Australia Clay as she has honored her father in his last days on this earth.
Father, we also lift up our missionaries into your care.
Thank you for sending out from our midst missionaries
>   to Albania where people have been torn by prejudice and violence,
>   to the hill tribes of Thailand where good health is only for the few,
>   to Kenya where children are taken off the street to have a home in a Baptist orphanage.

Father, use our mission offerings to spread your Word.
Demonstrate your love, and offer salvation through Jesus the Christ.
Strengthen these missionaries to
>   face rejection that is inevitable,
>   adapt to cultures that are strange to them,
>   develop friends in faraway places so they'll have someone to talk to when they are sad or frustrated,
>   sense your presence as they struggle with loneliness and heartache like all

the rest of us.
Minister to others as you have ministered to them.

We offer our prayers confident that you will respond,
    not as we anticipate,
        but in a miraculous way that will surprise and delight us. Amen.

A sermon about Mary and missionaries ~ December 11, 2011

Commissioning

*H*eavenly Father,
In your Word and through your prophets we learn of your promises.
We put our hopes in your promises of
> Eternal life,
> Abiding presence,
> Amazing grace.

We are especially mindful of your promised Holy Spirit for those who walk in grief, like Al Taylor and his family following the sudden death of Mary Taylor last week.
And for L.G. Hill and Donna Athas following the death of Ruby Hill the week before.
Your promise of resurrection is the one we cling to with every dermal cell in our hands.

God we also discover in your Word and hear from your prophets that your promises come with a call, a call to go.
You are the God who calls people like us: engineers, school teachers, IT specialists, designers, homemakers, nurses, soldiers, and counselors.

You call us to places like Haiti,
the poorest country in the Western Hemisphere,
to build houses and construct water purification units,
to walk among and work alongside of brothers and sisters
who know little of air conditioned churches and covered dish suppers,
to use our abundant resources with those who have little to nothing.

Father, we commission these servants of yours to go to Haiti
and look for Jesus Christ in the world,
and serve him, love him, and share with him.

We ask for protection from civil unrest.
We ask for success in homebuilding and presenting Christ to
the people of Ranquitte in a way that would honor Christ.
Allow us as a people to be obedient to our call while remaining here.
Lead us to be just as faithful in prayers for our brothers and sisters
in Haiti as those in Durham.
Give us hearts that reach out to others and take risks for the sake of the Gospel,
to enter the dangerous places, just as Jesus entered a dangerous place.

Continue to call, to provoke, to intrude, to bother us with your
hard, deep call to obedience,
Even as you promise eternal life, abiding presence, and amazing grace.
In Jesus' name, Amen.

Commissioning missionaries to go to Haiti ~ January 1, 2012

Parent-Child Covenant

Creator God,
Sovereign Lord, Creator of living DNA,
In your image you breathe souls into existence.
We bring these two infants as testimony of your power:
    Raleigh Ruth Brooks loaned to Aaron and Lorrie on September 2.
    Joel Chimezuru Uba gifted to Alexius and Cordelia Uba on November 11.
Give to each of these children
    fullness of life,
    homes filled with love,
    friends to run and play with in abundance,
    enough joy to keep them radiant,
    and enough sorrow to develop a sense of empathy for a world filled with sorrow.
Bring them into a saving and eternal relationship with Jesus Christ in accordance with your eternal grace and will.
Aid these mothers in recovery and give to these dads a deep-seated love for Mom and a patience for raising their little children.
These lives are sacred, holy, unique creations for which we have a part.
We come confessing we don't always deem life sacred.
We have cheapened life by putting economic figures on it.
We pause and cry and grieve more when the rich and powerful die
than the lowly and the lonely die.
We have become callous toward the violence and war and death that dominate our world.
We mostly shrug our shoulders when we read about deaths
    in Afghanistan,
    in the slums of Durham,
    in the schools of large cities,
    in the sweatshops in Thailand.
Father, forgive us for allowing the world to shape our understanding of life and death
instead of the Scriptures you have provided for us.
Father, give us an overwhelming sense of the sanctity of all life:
    of the old and young,
    the rich and poor,
    the foreigner and the neighbor,
    the friend and the enemy.
Teach us that all of these are yours, and we should cherish them because you do.
In the name of the one who died so that everyone might live,
Jesus Christ our Lord. Amen.

A sermon on the sanctity of life ~ November 18, 2011

Ordination

*H*eavenly Father,
We confess you to be the God who calls, who wills, who summons,
who has concrete ideas about our future,
and who calls us by name.
And we confess that we are resistant to your call on our lives,
afraid of the places you send us,
indoctrinated to seek status and privilege instead of service and lowliness,
preoccupied with our needs rather than your unfailing provision.
And so we resist, we run, we hide, we rationalize that surely you have not called us.
But you do call and you have called Kyle Bauman into the Gospel ministry,
So we pray to you, we call out to you, the one who calls out to us.

We pray tonight, Father of Jesus, God of the one who called little Samuel,
and old Moses, and virgin Mary, and Kyle of Indiana and Kansas and Duke,
That you give us a fresh vision of your call,
That you give our parents a willingness to let go of called sons and daughters,
That you fill up our seminaries and divinity schools with the brightest,
most effective people from our churches,
That you confront our individual freedom with your holy voice.

We thank you for calling Kyle Bauman from Indiana to Durham,
and into the future you are still disclosing.
We thank you for his parents who brought him to your temple, and for the old and blind Elis who took care of him there.
And we thank you that he gave heed to your voice and continues to listen with care for further instruction.
Father, as Kyle seeks to answer your call,
>   your call to preaching and proclamation,
>   your call to prayer and persevering faith,
>   your call to social justice and spiritual renewal,
>   give him ears to hear and hands to serve,
>   guard him against temptation and lead him to communities of support,
>   give him daily bread and nightly rest,
>   give him companions with whom he can share friendship and love,
>   and give him an unswerving, unwavering, unshakable confidence
>   in the Gospel of your Son Jesus Christ, and anointing of the Holy Spirit.

Send him out from here on your mission to reconcile all things on heaven and earth
>   by making peace through Christ's blood, shed on the cross. Amen.

Kyle Baumann's Ordination Service ~ May 13, 2012

Graduation

Heavenly Father,
Today we celebrate with graduates and their families
for all the places they have been,
the achievements they have accumulated,
the moments with friends and families that have been treasures.
And we declare all these good gifts are from you.

But now as they step into the future,
we confess we don't know the way to go.
The future is cloudy,
The way is uncertain,
The step before us is covered in darkness.

We don't know if you want us to go far away or stay nearby,
start to the left or return to the right.
We cry out for answers.
We seek your direction, but you remain elusive.
We struggle with our doubts, we struggle with your commands.
We wrestle with truth, we struggle with ourselves, we strain with you.

Oh God, do not let these graduates go without blessing them.
Do not let any of us leave today without your blessing,
   in our confusion and uncertainty,
   in our sin and cowardice.
   in our conniving and controlling,
Do not let us go.
Change us, mold us, wound us...but God do not leave us.

We desire to please you and worship you.
And we know that such desire pleases you and becomes worship.
We trust you to take our confusion and make it blessing,
We trust that you can and will convert our weakness into strength,
We trust that you will forgive us and make us new,
We trust that you can take wounded spirits and allow us to limp
into your future.
We don't know the future, but at least we know you.
And that is enough.
That is enough. In Jesus' name we pray.

Graduation Sunday ~ June 3, 2012

*H*eavenly Father,
You the creator, the giver of goodness, the maker of possibilities for achievement,
You have given, provided, helped, and sustained these graduates.
They are children of your bounty, sons and daughters of your grace.
As they move tassel from one side to the other, we corporately give thanks for parents:
> who taught them their first lessons in theology and ethics,
> who provided their first medical care,
> who acted as their servants when utterly helpless.

We give thanks for their teachers at school and church:
> who pushed them into mental and theological arenas of discomfort,
> who opened new doors so they might see more of your creation,
> who challenged them, perhaps coerced them, toward excellence.

We pray for their growth and well-being as they move into the future.
Protect them from evil, and equip them to confront evil in this world.
Give them eyes to see the plight of poverty throughout the world.
Give them hearts to care for others, especially those who receive little care.
Give them minds for great thoughts, serious solutions, and careful planning.
Empower them to become a part of a new generation of zealous servants for Christ.
Create in them a thirst for justice, a devotion to service, and a heart for purity.

Father, who overcomes our fear with utterances of courage,
> who overrides our scarcity with abundance,
> who takes the fish of the few to feed the many,
> who converts young women on the edge of adulthood
> into young women on the edge of greatness,

Our gratitude does not match your generosity,
But we are grateful,
For these graduating seniors, for all your gifts, and for your son Jesus Christ our Lord. Amen.
And all the people said, "Amen."

Graduation Sunday ~ June 5, 2011

The Ten Commandments

𝒜lmighty God,
You who are our commander. We pledge obedience to your commands,
And we look to Jesus, the incarnation of the divine Word,
to understand your words, to interpret your commands—
> Jesus, the one who kept Sabbath while breaking the rules of men,
> Jesus, the one who condemned adultery, but forgave the adulterous woman,
> Jesus, the one who was murdered, whose life was stolen,
> whose popularity and power were coveted,
> And yet he only offered life.
> He gave to those in need and used his power in ways the world couldn't understand.

We confess that we are overwhelmed and awed by Jesus,
> but we don't always follow him.

We continue to bear false witness against our neighbor when our neighbor makes us angry.
> We hide hate in our hearts, when our enemies are nearby.
> We covet what others have and what the media insists that we need.
> We love you when it's convenient and our neighbors when they love us first.

Forgive our demand that others follow your commands while we give ourselves a pass.
Forgive our lack of self-awareness, so glibly naming the faults of others, and so oblivious to our own.
And lead us to read, interpret, and obey your commands, these wonderful words of life, as Jesus did;
Grounded in love for you and love for our neighbor.
This is our persistent and constant prayer, in Jesus' name. Amen.

A sermon on Jesus' fulfillment of the 10 Commandments ~ October 23, 2011

*H*eavenly Father,
You are above us, beyond us, before us, and greater than we can express;
You are the God who created everything, including such monumental edifices as time, eternity, space, quarks, and atoms.
Our only knowledge of You comes from your gracious self-disclosure.
You have given us a tidbit of knowledge through your word.
You have stirred our hearts with your power in your creation,
And you have revealed yourself to us most perfectly through your Son.

Yet your Word is filtered through our words in our language,
Your creation must pass through the lens of our eyes,
Your Son only graced this planet for 33 years,
While your Spirit is more glorious than we can fathom.

So we bow down to you to worship, but not the Bible.
We gaze upon your creation with awe, but we don't worship it.
We come into this holy space to worship you, but we don't worship the space.
We worship you the Holy Other, the Tremendous Mystery, the Absolute Truth, the Perfect Love, the Heavenly Father, the only begotten Son, the Holy Spirit.

We come confessing our sin, which prevents us from full knowledge.
We are consumed with ourselves more than our neighbors.
We seek to please our neighbors more than you.
We try to give you some time in the midst of our busy schedules,
    rather than give you all of ourselves so you might control our schedules.
We arrogantly think you are on our side in the battle against evil,
    rather than humble ourselves in your midst in the face of our own evil.

So forgive our sin which drives us further away from you and our neighbor.
Cleanse us of unrighteousness that clogs our souls like bad cholesterol.
Give us a new Spirit grounded in the love of Christ, the compassion of Christ,
    and the goodness of Christ. Amen.

        A sermon on the second commandment ~ August 21, 2011

Eternal One,
We all cry, "Holy, Holy, Holy," for that is what you are, and so much more.
You are above us and beyond us in strength, moral goodness, love, and knowledge.
You are unutterable, beyond expression, so different from us.
We dare not speak your name, except that you give us permission.
You have graced us, surprised us, frightened us, by giving us your Name.

But God, we have abused your name.
We have spoken it much too casually.
We have used it among speech that is evil, profane, and frivolous.
We have used your name to get us somewhere, to move ahead, to entertain,
Instead of the fearful and reverent acts of prayer, praise, and proclamation.

Forgive us, Holy One, for unholy speech.
Forgive us for abusing your name.
Forgive us for being casual about your name and your call on our lives.
Forgive us for not taking your name seriously.
Bring us back to your holy mountain, where you abide.
Allow us to dare glimpse at your backside,
And speak your name,
And hear your commands for covenant living,
And receive your costly forgiveness,
which comes at no price less than life and blood.

Today, O God, call us again,
To be your children, to be your sons and daughters,
To come before your presence,
To speak and pray as Jesus the Messiah taught us to pray by saying,
Our Father, who art in heaven; hallowed by thy name;
Thy kingdom come, thy will be done, on earth as it is in heaven.
Give us this day, our daily bread.
And forgive us our trespasses, as we forgive those who trespass against us.
And lead us not into temptation, but deliver us from evil.
For thine is the kingdom and the power and the glory, forever, Amen.

A sermon on God's Name ~ August 28, 2011

*H*eavenly Father,
Maker of heaven and earth, creator of sea and sky,
    Governor of night and day,
        Miraculous worker of creating swimming, crawling and flying things,
        Perfect scientist, making humankind in your image from nothing more than dirt.
And then you rested. You ceased. You gazed upon that which you created.
And you called it good—very good.
Then you commanded us to rest. To cease, rejoice, play, relax.
You have liberated us from the bondage of slavery and given us rest.
You have freed us from the burden of unceasing productivity.
You have made us more than workers, laborers, producers, consumers.
We are children, sons, daughters, friends, lovers, dancers, sleepers.
We thank you, O God, for the gift of Sabbath,
for the freedom it brings, the rest it provides, the dignity it summons.
We thank you for a Lord's Day,
    a day of remembering Jesus' resurrection,
    a day for worship, study, reflection, prayer, fellowship, and fun,
    a day for gathering as a community and celebrating our life in you,
    a day for encouraging one another to live this new life you've worked to create,
    a day for us to rejuvenate us so that we might enjoy your blessings.
But God, we have not always observed your Sabbath.
We confess we forget you are the creator, and not us.
We confess we have tried to work 7 days a week, instead of 6.
We have allowed the world to define us in its hurried, chaotic image,
So that we see ourselves as producers, laborers, and consumers only.
And we have forsaken the Lord's Day.
    We complained about the music.
    It was too contemporary or traditional,
        or we had to stand up too long.
And so we stopped worshiping You, our creator.

We got bored with the preaching.
It was too academic or simplistic or liberal or conservative.
And so we stopped listening for your Spirit.
Someone hurt our feelings. They didn't acknowledge our contribution.
And so we withdrew from the body of Christ.
And so we come today Father, tired, bored, irritated, and hurt.
And we need your comfort, your correction, your sustaining grace to help us through.
We need joy and excitement and peace, and of course, rest.
So give us your peace and joy and rest. Let it be sufficient for the week. Amen.
        A sermon on Sabbath ~ September 4, 2011

*A*lmighty God,
Maker of heaven and earth, converter of chaos into order,
Creator of man and woman;
In your divine wisdom you have bestowed a gift upon every human,
excepting Adam and Eve.
You have given each person a mother and father;
Until our recent tampering with your biosphere, there has always been a mother and father for each child.
And how we need both.
Our mothers and fathers have been our teachers,
    teaching us about commandments and cars and cooking.
They have been our nurturers,
    preparing us for kindergarten, and college, and cloudy days.
They have been our rebukers,
    revealing our wrong when no one else loved us enough to do it.
They have been our forgivers,
    opening their arms after we have snubbed them, and opening their doors after we have run away like a prodigal.
They have been our doctors,
    reducing our fevers, prescribing medicines, and staying nearby when we were throwing up.
Father, you have called us to honor them, respect them, remember them.
And so we do—at least we want to; but we need your help.
So help us honor them
    by living a life pleasing to God,
    by speaking words of kindness and respect to them,
    by obeying their instructions,
    by caring for them in their old age and nurturing their dignity.

Forgive us when we dishonor them, and forgive them when they
    provoke us,
    neglect us, abuse us,
    manipulate us,
    attempt to control us,
    and use us for their egocentric impulses.

Give both of us, parent and child, a godly and biblical sense of relationship.
Give parents the capacity to love without ceasing, and children the capacity to honor without reserve.
And when one or both of us fails, forgive us, help us to forgive one another, and begin a new day, a new life in relationships, as you intended from the start.
Father, let us begin today and leave this sanctuary with a new commitment of loving our children and honoring our parents. Amen.

        A sermon on honoring father and mother ~ September 11, 2011

O God,
It is March Madness. A disease has swept over your people, and they are delusional.
It is a season where hopes are being dashed, and dreams are being shattered.
There are upsets, and people are upset.
So much time and energy has been invested in the season, and now this.
All were hoping for glory and coming to the end of the rainbow to find their pot of gold.
But so many have experienced only loss and tears and disbelief.
It is a time of March Madness. Your people have committed adultery.

Husbands have forsaken wives in pursuit of temporary pleasures.
Wives have forsaken husbands trying to find that spark that once kindled fire.
Young people are pursuing passions that are intense but fleeting:
Internet, pornography, office parties, neighborhood trysts.
O God, we are an adulteress people.

And therefore we are unfaithful to you. We have turned our backs on you.
We even blame you for our infidelity:
> Why did you make us like this?
> Why did you give us passions?
> Why did you do this, O God?

Forgive us, Heavenly Father. Forgive us thou who has created us and given sacred passion to us. Give to us a pure heart so that we might see you.
Cleanse our minds from that which is unclean, and bring to focus the beauty of a long, glorious, and wonderful relationship with you.
Reveal to us the beauty of Christ so that our hearts might be melted.
Show us your grace which is greater than our sin.
Give us hope which is greater than our despair.
Build our faith so that it might overcome our unfaithfulness.

And let us move from faith in you to faithfulness to our husbands and wives.
Rekindle the sanctity of marital intimacy where true love blooms.
Direct the passions you have given us toward the one who wears our wedding ring.
And may the joy of fidelity, love, intimacy, and security satisfy our longings.
Bring our ultimate longings for adventure, love, rapture, and delight
to the one who loved us enough to suffer, bleed, and die that we might love forever,
love with passion, and love completely.
Bring this March Madness to an end, where we can celebrate being in the Final Four,
In loving harmony with you, Father, Son, and Holy Ghost. Amen.

A sermon on the 7th Commandment ~ March 7, 2004

*H*eavenly Father,
You are the God from whom no lie can be hid,
and we are a people who tell many lies.
We lie to our parents because we know our actions are forbidden by them,
and we are trying to hide.
We lie to our children because we want to appear better than we really are,
and we are trying to hide.
We lie to our employees and employers because we want to protect our jobs and our profits,
and we are trying to hide.
We are like Isaiah the prophet, men and women of unclean lips, and we live among a people of unclean lips.
And still, when we come into holy, truthful presence, we are exposed.
We cannot hide. We want to hide. We don't want to hide.
For you, O God, are a God of truth.
You speak truth to power, for you are unafraid of militaries and political alliances.
You speak truth in love, for you care for us and are compassionate toward us.
You speak truth through truth, for your son was the way, the truth, and the life,
And only through him can we come to you,
Only through Jesus can we experience truth in its fullness.
So God we ask you with trembling, reluctant, anxious hearts,
To touch our lips with the coals of white, hot, truth.
Cleanse our tongues and make us a people who speak truth.
Overcome our insecurities with your grace so that we might
Spread encouragement instead of rumors.
Lead us to walk away from gossip instead of bask in its decay.
Help us to see that truth-telling brings peace with ourselves and peace with you.
For Satan is the Father of lies, and you are the Creator, Sustainer, and Incarnation of Truth.
In the name of the One who is the Truth, Jesus our Lord.

A sermon on the 9th Commandment ~ March 29, 2004

Marriage and Human Sexuality

*H*eavenly Father,
In the beginning you made man and woman,
> Similar but different;
>> One wanted to be admired, one wanted to be cherished.
And you made these two, one;
Two bodies but one flesh,
A mystery like Christ and the church are mysterious bride and groom.

Your call is to love, cherish, protect, and serve till death do us part.
We confess today we have fallen short of that command.
> Love is patient, but we lovers are not always patient.
> Love is kind, but we are not always kind to our mates.
> Love is not proud, but sometimes our pride gets in the way of our loving.
> Love does not keep a record of wrongs, and yet we can turn a tape recorder in our heads and replay again and again the hurts we have received.
> Love is not easily angered, and yet we can lose our tempers over the smallest of slights.

So forgive us our sins as we forgive those who sin against us,
   even when the sinner is our spouse.
And teach us a new way to live, a Christ way to live.
Help us to think and act like a Christian at home with our spouses.
Teach us how to love one another while fully aware of the other's faults.
Help us to show grace when it would be more natural to offer punishment,
Lead us to care for the spouse you have entrusted to us,
   as much as we care for our houses, our mortgages, and our jobs.

Lead us, O God, to become virtuous followers of Christ,
> who put on love,
>> which binds all virtue together in perfect unity. Amen.

A sermon on marriage ~ June 7, 2015

*A*lmighty God,
Creator of heaven and earth, sky and sea, man and woman,
You have given us the command to be fruitful and increase and subdue the earth.
You have fashioned us anatomically to do this,
And because of our original and ongoing sin you have given us laws,
Laws to govern relationships, marriage, sexuality.
In the fullness of time Jesus came and fulfilled these laws,
so that we might see how they are to be acted out in his person.
He obeyed the law and exposed the failure of others to obey the law.
Then your servant Paul wrote letters to churches to explain this
new fulfillment of the law through Christ;
He gave us instructions that we deem holy, sacred, and eternal.

But we don't always understand the law and we need guidance;
Sometimes we do understand it and just don't like it.
It is contrary to desires, it inhibits our impulses, it challenges our behavior,
And so we pick and choose which parts we obey.
We pick and choose which parts we demand others obey.
We all stand guilty, under condemnation, because we act out these impulses.

So forgive us this day, Creator, Law-Giver, Judge,
Remove our guilt and replace it with righteousness.
Take off our blinders and give us a pure vision of Christ.

And help us use our human sexuality in the boundaries of your Law.
Take this wild, volatile, passionate flame
and subdue it, bridle it, control it.
Then unleash it within the context of holy relationships
so that its powers and passions can be used
for good, beautiful, life-giving purposes,
that can be enjoyed, cherished, and valued.
In the name of Jesus, we pray, Amen

A sermon on human sexuality ~ April 22, 2012

O God,
In the beginning you created the heavens and the earth;
You created male and female, and the first commandment you gave to them was
"Be fruitful and multiply."
And it was good, very good.
Your command and gift to be sexually intimate was one of your gifts
to be cherished, protected, and used for purposes
    of making babies and making intimacy.

But this gift has been abused, maligned, ignored, and corrupted.
It has been used outside the covenant relationship.
It has been used as a form of power and manipulation and unholy lust.

Now we are living with the judgment of our sinfulness,
    emotional disconnection,
    feelings of emptiness,
    addictions to fantasies,
    neglect of the real needs of our mates,
    pregnancies when people are unprepared for parenthood,
    abortions to cover our tracks.
And the world has applauded as we have moved farther and farther away
    from your wonderful plans for this gift.

We have been unfaithful to you.
We have turned our backs on you.
We even blame you for our infidelity.
    Why did you make us like this?
    Why did you give us passions?
    Why did you do this, O God?

Forgive us, Heavenly Father.
Give to us a pure heart so that we might see you.
Show us your grace which is greater than our sin.
Give us hope which is greater than our despair.
Build our faith so that it might overcome our unfaithfulness.

God, help us move from faith in you, to faithfulness to our husbands and wives.
Rekindle the sanctity of marital intimacy where true love blooms.
Direct the passions you have given us toward the one who wears our wedding ring.
And may the joy of fidelity, love, intimacy, and security, satisfy our longings.
Bring our ultimate longings for adventure, love, rapture, and delight
    to the one who loved us enough to suffer, bleed, and die
        that we might love forever,
        love with passion,

and love completely.

Bring us to the point where we might live
in loving harmony with you, O God. In Jesus' name. Amen.

A sermon on human sexuality ~ May 3, 2015

Community Senior Citizens Ministry

Almighty God,
Maker of heaven and earth, author of dignity for every human being,
We acknowledge your wisdom, revealed and understood throughout the world by people of varied traditions, nationalities, and ethnicities.
Today, we want to thank you for providing every generation with elders, mentors, and
sages to guide our paths and remind us of what matters the most.

These elders in our midst have been our teachers,
    teaching us about love, mercy, and justice.
They have been our nurturers,
    preparing us for kindergarten, and college, and cloudy days.
They have been our prophets,
    exposing the injustices in our world, even when it puts their lives in peril.
They have been our doctors and nurses,
    reducing our fevers, prescribing our medicines, healing our wounds.

God, you have called us to honor them, respect them, and remember them.
And so we promise to do this—at least we want to.
What we do at and through the Shepherd's Center is part of that sacred promise.
    So help us honor them by speaking to them words of kindness and respect,
    Empower us to care for them when they are
sick, cold, lonely, and unsure they are visible to anyone.
    Help us to honor them in their old age by nurturing their dignity and aiding their health.
    Help us as people of varied faiths to hold their dignity up before a mirror
    so they might be reminded of their true selves, your beloved children.

Take The Shepherd's Center and make it a vessel for the health and wholeness
    of our aged brothers and sisters,
Multiply our efforts so that all of Winston Salem can join in these divine efforts to love our senior population with
    diligent hands,
    eager minds,
    and compassionate voices.
I pray this in Jesus' name. Amen.

        Opening Prayer for the Shepherd's Center ~ March 19, 2013

Mother's Day

*H*eavenly Father,
You are the God of our mothers,
    some of them long gone and treasured;
    some of them very present and lovable;
    some of them far away, yet near to our hearts.

You are the God of our grandmothers
    and many other mothers whose lives
    are shaping us beyond our understanding.
You are also the God of those who yearn to be mothers,
    but have never given birth;
    women who prayed Hannah's prayer,
    but didn't receive the same answer.
Today we pray that you comfort them
    as they live with maternal instincts
    that must turn toward others' children.

You are the God of our mothers and grandmothers,
    who are no longer living on earth.
Many of us have heavy hearts today because we miss them so much.
    Comfort us with your Spirit;
    Give us your Presence as we honor them with our memories.

You are the God of those whose mothers were
    absent, neglectful, even abusive.
We still bear these scars of that history.
    so heal us, and let us become wounded healers.

You are the God of mothers whose children have died,
    in the womb, just out of the womb, in the world.
And today the pain is deep and the loss is overwhelming,
    So wrap your arms around us, just like we would
    wrap our arms around our children if we could.

Be a mother to us, O God;
Bandage the scrapes to our souls;
Wipe the tears from our eyes;
Catch us when we fall off the swing;
Smile at us, when no one else notices us.
Be a mother to us, O God. We need you today. Amen.

May 10, 2015

*H*eavenly Father,
We are a people deeply rooted in miracles before us;
Our faith is centered in Jesus Christ,
and yet it is his followers who have brought us to him.
Frequently, our mothers first brought us to him.
> They carried us to church where teachers told us that Jesus loved us.
> They sang songs to us affirming the message and truth of the Bible.
> They cared for us when we were sick, as if we were Jesus.
> They fed us when we were hungry, as if we were Jesus.
> And they suffered when we suffered, as if we were Jesus.

So today we give you thanks for mothers who have shaped us.
We thank you for mothers whose lives are recorded in your written word,
So our stories can be discovered in their stories.
> For mothers like Hannah, who committed her son to your care,
> For Elizabeth, who carried a kicking cousin of Jesus in her womb,
> For Sarah, who laughed when God gave her a child in old age,
> For Eunice, who planted faith into her son, preparing him for missionary service.

Father, give us today a deep and abiding respect for these servants of yours.
Keep us from dishonoring them, neglecting them, or dismissing their contribution to our lives.
Forgive us when we sin against you by dishonoring them.
Forgive us for listening to the secular voices of cynicism more than the faithful voices of these women.
May our lives reflect their goodness and yield to their teachings derived from you.
Expand our love for our mothers and increase our faith in your Son.

In the name of Mary's son, Jesus, Amen.

Sermon: "Eunicious" ~ 2 Timothy 2:1-5 ~ May 13, 2012

INDEPENDENCE DAY

Don Gordon

Heavenly Father,
God of peace, God of Justice, God of freedom,
We give you thanks for your cadences of freedom most especially on this day;
Cadences that have surged through the lives of
Washington, Madison, and Jefferson,
and those of Jesus, Paul, and Timothy,
and those lesser known Baptists Helwys, Williams, Leland, and Hobbs;
For those who defended the state from enemies
Bradley, Eisenhouer, Powell, and Shelton;
For those defenders connected by blood to this congregation
Gaddis, Hahn, and Hodge;
And all those nameless risk-takers who infiltrate into evil lands
to rescue the innocent and constrain the evil.
Deliver us from amnesia concerning the liberty that is ours
and the great strength and voice it takes to maintain liberty.
Deliver us from amnesia and help us to remember the words of Jesus
who told us to honor Caesar and God, but always but God first.
Deliver us from amnesia and help us to remember the words of the first Baptists,
who told us not to depend on the state to do the work of the church.
Deliver us from amnesia and help us to remember the evil latent within
all humans, and the need to limit anyone's power however noble they seem.

And we pray for our neighbors in other countries where religious liberty
is stifled under the oppressive hand of tyranny.
We pray for our brothers in prison in Iraq,
For the churches under terror from ISIS in Syria,
For pastors whose lives are constantly threatened in North Korea,
For sisters worshipping in secret Mynamar.

God, unleash your Spirit so all the world will hear the cadence of liberty.
Let freedom rush through earth's veins
So we can genuinely choose you, choose life, and choose good over evil.
God bless Ardmore Baptist Church,
God bless America,
And God lead Ardmore Baptist Church and America to be a blessing to you
and all the nations on the face of your earth.
In Jesus' name, Amen.

A sermon on Baptist history and freedom ~ July 5, 2015

Homecoming

100 ☦ Don Gordon

𝒜lmighty God,
    God of Abraham, Isaac, and Jacob;
    God of Sarah, Rebekah, and Rachel;
    God of Matthew Yates, Ray Hodge, and Ron Cumby;
    God of Mary Cole, J.R. Pickett, and Edney Rigsbee;
We proclaim the mighty deeds you have done in our midst.
We remember the favor you have shown to your people.
We have been saved for your namesake, to make your name known.

On this day of Homecoming we remember our past and your providence.
You took a $30 acre of land and created a Baptist church.
You gave us the name of a great missionary so we would remember to
be missionaries.
You called preachers to exalt the name of Jesus.
You inspired SS teachers to lift up the Bible for instruction and guidance.
You compelled us to give so missionaries could go to other countries.
You led us to support the young, college students, and divinity school students
    so they would have a safe, loving, home base from which to grow.
You have inspired us to serve as Jesus served, and so we have cooked, cleaned,
built, and organized for the advancement of this church and the glory of the
kingdom of God.

God, we confess our history also includes infidelity, casualness, and selfishness.
We have had times in our corporate and personal history when we have been
slack in our commitment, seduced by modern gods, satisfied with mediocrity,
and short in patience. We have loved the world too much and you too little.

We stand before you in remorse and repentance, fully aware we have let you
down.
So forgive us and create a right spirit within us,
    a spirit of generosity, gentleness, graciousness, gladness of heart.
Send us out from this place, not only well-fed and happy,
but dedicated to our call to be ambassadors for Christ,
as though you were making your appeals to the world through us.
Impress on us, that as ambassadors every word we speak, every action we take,
every dollar we spend is a reflection on you, your church, and our Savior.

Help us, O Lord, make a greater impact on Durham for Jesus' sake,
fill us with your Spirit for the world's sake, so that every man, woman,
and child will know of your great deeds and your matchless love.
We pray to you Father, in the name of your Son, in the power of your Spirit.
Amen.

Homecoming at Yates Baptist Church ~ 2010

Organ Dedication

Almighty God,

In the beauty of this sanctuary, itself set apart for the worship of your Holy and Loving Being, we do now offer our praises to you both now and forevermore. We bow before your Presence in fear and trembling because you are an awesome God, and your power is infinite. And yet we come completely trustful because we know you love us with tender compassion and great mercy. So accept our feeble efforts of worship and listen now to our songs that exalt your name and the name of your Son, Jesus Christ our Lord.

We beseech thee, that as we dedicate this marvelous instrument of music to your glory and honor, that it will always be used for that sacred purpose and for nothing less. May the sounds of music that arise from it be like the aroma of pleasing offerings that give expression to hearts intent on loving mercy, justice and humility. May the voices that join in harmony with these musical sounds expose a sincere love for you and the neighbors you bring into our lives. May the joining of instrument and voice in worship here inspire greater confidence in your eternal purposes and a greater desire to follow Jesus Christ more closely. And may those who appreciate beautiful music, but do not know our Savior, be cut to the heart by your Spirit, so that they may repent, turn from their lostness, and come to a saving, life-changing knowledge of Jesus Christ.

Thank you, O God, for the granting of these petitions that are in keeping with your will. We are grateful that you have loved us enough to allow us to participate in your redemptive plans for the universe through the act of authentic worship and personal witness.

Consecrate us, our voices, our talents, and the gift of this organ to that sacred task from this point until that glorious day in the Eternal Kingdom, when we shall join the choir of heaven in singing, "Hallelujah! The Lord God Almighty reigns! Let us rejoice and be glad and give him glory! For the wedding of the Lamb has come and his bride has made herself ready."
In Jesus' Name, Amen.

June 25, 2000

Dedication of Town Library

*O*mniscient God, Giver of life and source of all knowledge, we have gathered here today as a community to seek your blessings on this library and to publicly profess our belief that learning is a sacred act of faith. We stand and speak with one voice to dedicate these walls, books, videos, computers, and magazines to the sacred pursuit of knowledge.

We stand together hoping that Hispanic parents will find here tools to help them adapt to a different culture and community.

We stand together hoping that senior adults will find moments of satisfaction and relaxation as they integrate their life experiences with the classical authors of Western Civilization.

We stand together hoping that parents will find here resources for nurturing their families' intellectual growth in a world dominated by MTV and 9-second sound bites.

We stand here hoping that this place will keep alive forever the indomitable spirit of Dr. Steele and his passion for creating an academic refuge for every community.

We stand here hoping that moral education creates moral communities.

And so we dedicate not only these walls of Sheetrock and these sheets of prose to the future of this community, but more importantly we dedicate ourselves to the spirit of Dr. Steele and to the spirit of creating space in every community for reading, thinking, reflecting, and dreaming. We dedicate ourselves to supporting the efforts of this library, reading to our children, fostering a community of reasoned love and love for reason. We dedicate ourselves to not giving up on any future generation and therefore giving the tools that will enable them to fulfill the constitutional dream of every American throughout this nation's history—the pursuit of life, liberty, and happiness.

We pray this prayer with one united voice encompassing every race and economic station in life, in the name of the one who called himself the way, the truth and the life, Jesus Christ my Lord. Amen.

Dedication of Steele Memorial Library in Mount Olive, NC ~ May 19, 1996

PRESIDENTIAL INAUGURATION

*P*resident-elect Barack Obama has asked Rick Warren, Senior Pastor of Saddleback Church in Lake Forest, California, to give the invocation at his inauguration this year. This selection has drawn criticism from the left fringe of the Democratic Party because of Warren's views on social issues of gay marriage and abortion. I have reflected on this selection and thought about what I would pray if I were asked to pray at this inauguration. Here is the prayer I published in our church newsletter for our new president:

Almighty and Everlasting God of the Ages,
This day demands that we praise you, for the day is yours, not ours.
We could not live this day without reference to you,
> your gifts
> your providence
> your power.

You and you alone made the heavens and the earth.
You and you alone decree what is just and execute ultimate judgment.
You and you alone set the prisoners free, give sight to the blind, and raise the dead.
You and you alone uphold the weak, supply the poor, cry out for the oppressed.

But then you call a person—a boy, a girl, a man, a woman—to stand in your stead, to speak your words, to enact your justice.
You send a baby down the Nile to confront a Pharaoh.
You send an old man on a mission to start a nation to bless the world.
You send a boy into battle to face a giant.
You send your son to redeem this world's brokenness.

And in this great experiment we call The United States of America,
You have sent farmers and lawyers and soldiers—both common and uncommon—to offer leadership, execute justice, and defend the constitution created by our parents.
Today, in your providential sovereignty, you have given us Barack Hussein Obama to lead this nation and carry the flag of liberty for all the world to witness. So we pray for
President Obama as he steps into the fray of battle against incalcitrant powers, wars and rumors of wars across the world, economic uncertainties, and the scars of this nation's past sins.

Give him a voice to confront pharaohs so the oppressed might be liberated.
Give him a confidence to face the Goliaths of racism, injustice, and addictions to violence so they might be defeated.
Give him a vision to see the possibilities of new blessings, ideas, and freedoms in a world conditioned to protect the few at the expense of the many.
Bless him so that he might bless the world.

We also pray for ourselves, we the people of this abundantly blessed land, that we will support and pray for our president, his family, and his administration; that we will live up to the ideals we hold for ourselves and others; that we will place no greater burden on our President than we are willing to carry ourselves.

And that we will join him in seeking peace,
- acting with wisdom,
- helping the weak,
- promoting freedom,
- increasing civility,
- acting morally,
- and establishing justice for all.

We pray this in the name of the Father, Son, and Holy Spirit, Amen.

January 2009

The Charleston Massacre

Don Gordon

Almighty God,
We come before your throne of grace with many petitions and praises.
We are asking for your providential care for our mission teams
    in Belize and in the Ukraine.
We are thanking you for fathers who lead their homes to be
    places of safety, faithfulness, and love.
We are seeking your guidance to walk paths of righteousness
    in the arena of sexual intimacy.

But today, O God, I feel compelled to pray for my
    brothers and sisters in Charleston, S.C.
Evil has penetrated the walls of your church,
    under the guise of a curious prayer partner,
    and then death and destruction erupted.

God, our hearts are broken for our family in Charleston,
    and so we ask that you bind up the brokenhearted,
    send your balm of healing,
    and meet death and the devil with Jesus Christ's
    love, perseverance, and resurrection.
Bring us together as a nation, and use your church to
    promote healing,
    defeat racism,
    unite all races in the common pursuit of peace and justice,
    and protect the innocent.
Lead us, as your church, not to be silent in the face of evil,
But to speak your truth with grace,
To confront evil with the greater power of love.
Convert our good intentions into words
    and our words into action,
    and our action into your redemptive plans.
    And teach us to pray as Jesus prayed....

The Sunday after the Charleston slayings ~ June 21, 2015

Invocations

Almighty God,
All praise to you, O King Divine, for you did yield the glory that was rightly yours, as you came to us in lowliness and humility in the form of flesh and blood. You came as a servant obedient unto death, even death on a cross. We have come, therefore, to join the angels of heaven in exalting the name of Jesus, to confess with one accord that Jesus is Lord, and to bow before His presence in humility and rightful honor.

Open our eyes to the truth of Jesus.

Open our ears to the suffering cries of this world.

And open our hearts to a new and clearer understanding of who you are.

In Jesus' name. Amen.

Almighty God,

With glad and grateful hearts we gather as the body of Christ on this Lord's day. We are glad because we are in your presence. We are grateful because we have been redeemed by the blood of Jesus Christ and given new life through him.

O God, we are in such dire need of a fresh touch by your Spirit. Send your Spirit and topple the idols that seek to sap our strength. May we leave here to rise anew, holy, pleasing, and pure in your sight, to witness of Jesus Christ for the rest of the world.

Amen.

Almighty God,

Who can question you? Who has an arm like you that can hurl the planets into orbit and bring intelligent life from a seed and an egg? Who can take the life of a self-absorbed yuppie and transform him into an unselfish servant for all humankind? Who can speak in every language that has ever been created from English to Ebonics, from Latin to Arabic, from German to Swahili? And still speak the universal language of the heart?

O God, we know you can do all things, even that which we, in our arrogant modern minds, deem impossible. No plan of yours is ultimately thwarted.

And so we come today to hear your plans, to hear words from the plan book, and sing songs of praise to the Grand Planner. We are here to reverently and fearfully utter your name and call on you to save us, forgive us, control us, and show us your plan. Open the minds of all who have dared approached your holiness and lead us as we worship you.

In the Holy Name of Jesus, Amen.

Heavenly Father,
Our delight is in thee, our joy is made complete in thee, our lives find meaning and purpose in thee; for you are our Creator who formed us in the womb and continue to give us sustenance for living. You are the One with whom we are in covenant relationship by giving your Son Jesus to us and for us. We in turn offer now, in these brief moments, our lives and hearts to you in worship. So cleanse our worship from any impurities and accept it as our sacrifice to thee, O Lord, our God and our Redeemer.
In Jesus' name, Amen.

Almighty God,

We praise you today. We praise you in your sanctuary; we praise you for your mighty deeds and for your exceeding greatness.

We praise you this morning with the sound of the pipe organ and the voices of young children. We praise you with our voices in triumphant song and prayers from lips, which continually battle uncleanness.

Open our minds to the truth of your Word today, speak to our hearts directly through the power of your Holy Spirit, and cleanse us of the obstructions in our lives that prevent us from experiencing the full measure of Christ's love and peace. Through Christ we pray, Amen

*H*osanna in the Highest,
Blessed be the name of our Lord.
You are our God, the God of Abraham, Isaac, and Jacob,
The God who chooses the old and feeble to create the living and powerful.
You are the God of Sarah, Rebekah, and Rachel,
The God who chooses the weak and barren to reveal strength and vitality.
Hosanna, blessed be the name of the Lord.
You are the God revealed in Jesus Christ, true God and true man,
Born of the spirit in the womb of a virgin.
Hosanna in the highest. We sing our praise to you today,
on this side of the river.
But one day, one day soon,
We are bound to cross the river and sing hosannas
in the choirs of heaven.
Hosanna in the highest. Blessed be the name of the Lord.
Amen.

About the Author

Don Gordon has served as the pastor of Ardmore Baptist Church in Winston-Salem, North Carolina since 2013. Prior to that, he served as a pastor at churches in Durham, Mount Olive, and Spruce Pine, North Carolina; and Emporia, Virginia. He and his wife Elizabeth have been married since 1985 and have three daughters: Sarah, Hannah, and Rebekah.

He earned a Doctorate of Ministry degree from Columbia Theological Seminary (PCUSA), an M.Div. from Southeastern Baptist Theological Seminary, and a B.S. degree in Mathematics from Campbell University, where he was a four-year letterman in tennis. He did further graduate studies in Mathematics at N.C. State University. Currently he is serving on the Board of Trustees for Campbell University and the Board of Directors for The Baptist Center for Ethics in Nashville, Tennessee.

Dr. Gordon's first book, *Like Drops of Morning Dew: A Concise History of North Carolina Baptists*, was published by the Baptist State Convention of North Carolina and distributed to its 3,800 churches. His second book, *Psalms for Children*, is an illustrated telling of 25 Psalms in words that are easy for children to understand. It is available in both trade paperback and hardcover from Prospective Press. *Prayers of a Pastor*, Dr. Gordon's third book, is a selection of prayers spanning a breadth of topics and distilled from his years of ministry.

An ACC basketball fan for life, Dr. Gordon enjoys playing, watching, and coaching a number of sports, particularly basketball and tennis.

www.ingramcontent.com/pod-product-compliance
Lightning Source LLC
Chambersburg PA
CBHW021154080526
44588CB00008B/332